What population sizes are most preferable? What are the population issues confronting the world today? How does population growth affect environment and economics?

These are the major issues confronted in *Population Change, Modernization, and Welfare*. The book shows you how to think intelligently about population and development problems. It gives you a succinct but complete overview of the impact of population movements both upon man's welfare and upon modernization of developing countries, together with treatment of the politico-economic policies called for.

It reviews both the past and the prospective growth of world population and shows how the impact of population growth upon man's environment affects income-producing capacity.

The book stresses an economic point of view. It covers the world-wide economic aspects of population growth based on the most recent research findings and studies. The problems are serious and will become increasingly critical if ignored in the future. *Population Change, Modernization, and Welfare* brings you up-to-date and gives you the background for forming your own conclusions and solutions. You are made aware of the costs, benefits, and net effects of population growth and can consider the problems with intelligence and imagination.

Joseph Spengler, Ph.D., Ohio State University, is the author of *France Faces Depopulation, French Predecessors of Malthus, Population Economics,* and *Indian Economic Thought.*

Prentice-Hall, Inc., Englewood Cliffs, N.J.

Population

Change,

Modernization,

and

Welfare

JOSEPH SPENGLER Duke University

Library of Congress Cataloging in Publication Data

SPENGLER, JOSEPH JOHN
    Population change, modernization, and welfare.

    (Modernization of traditional societies series)
    Bibliography: p.
    1. Population. 2. Underdeveloped areas—Population.
I. Title. II. Series.
HB871.S6518   301.32   73–17130
ISBN 0–13–687152–6
ISBN 0–13–687145–3 (pbk.)

To the memory of Charles E. Ferguson
and Robert S. Smith, economists and friends

10 9 8 7 6 5 4 3 2 1

Printed in the United States of America

PRENTICE-HALL INTERNATIONAL, INC., London
PRENTICE-HALL OF AUSTRALIA, PTY. LTD., Sydney
PRENTICE-HALL OF CANADA, LTD., Toronto
PRENTICE-HALL OF INDIA PRIVATE LIMITED, New Delhi
PRENTICE-HALL OF JAPAN, INC., Tokyo

WILBERT E. MOORE / NEIL J. SMELSER, Editors

Modernization of Traditional Societies Series

Contents

Tables

The twentieth century will be called many things by future historians—the Age of Global War, perhaps, the Age of Mass Society, the Age of the Psychoanalytic Revolution, to name a few possibilities. One name that historians certainly will not fail to give our century is the Age of the New Nation. For, evidently, the convulsive emergence of the colonies into independence and their subsequent struggle to join the ranks of the prosperous, powerful, and peaceful is the most remarkable revolution of our time. Taking the world as a whole, men are now preoccupied with no subject more than they are with the travail of the New Nations. The world of the social sciences has been studying the pace of social change in these newly emergent areas, and from time to time has been engaging in technical assistance and even in the giving of advice on high levels of social strategy. Little of this effort has reached publicly accessible form. Though technical treatises abound, and isolated, journalistic reports of distinctly exotic countries are not wanting, college curricula have scarcely reflected either the scientific endeavors or the world-wide revolutions in technology and in political affairs.

This series on "Modernization of Traditional Societies" is designed to inform scholars, students, and citizens about the way quiet places have come alive, and to introduce at long last materials on the contemporary character of developing

EDITORIAL FOREWORD   areas into college curricula for the

thought leaders of the near future. To these ends we have assembled experts over the range of the social sciences and over the range of the areas of the underdeveloped and newly developing sections of the earth that were once troublesome only to themselves.

We are proud to be participants in this series, and proud to offer each of its volumes to the literate world, with the hope that that world may increase, prosper, think, and decide wisely.

WILBERT E. MOORE
NEIL J. SMELSER

Numbers have always been of great concern to men who were conscious of their membership in the same political or quasipolitical group, first because safety consisted largely in numbers, then because output of goods and services long depended almost entirely upon the number of workmen, which depended upon the group or nation's population. Those concerned with population questions almost invariably focused their attention upon the state or nation. This was true of early Chinese and Indian writers, of Plato and Aristotle, and particularly of writers during the emergence of nation-states and mercantilist economic policy and on into the nineteenth century. Only since World War II has the matter of population come to be examined in a world as well as a national context. Of course some early writers were interested in the implications of population growth for international trade and the distribution of politico-military power (in the 1920s a League of Low-Birth-Rate Nations was proposed), but the point of departure of these discussions usually was the nation-state.

This study is primarily of the world-wide economic aspects of population growth, expressed in terms applicable to various parts of the world. Most of the data are presented in terms of the states of the world political order, partly because data are available only for individual states instead of for the world as a whole, partly because nearly all our information about relevant empirical relationships is based on studies of individual states. I emphasize relationships between demographic and socio-economic variables because these are the relationships that make the population question the most important confronting many nations and the world as a whole. Policies designed to alleviate population problems must be based upon these relations.

We shall review past and prospective world population growth, population distribution, and issues of population policy in Chapters 1 and 2. We shall deal with the impact of population growth upon man's environment in Chapter 3 and Chapter 5 (where we examine input costs of population growth). In Chapter 4 we shall discuss changes in age composition and the effects of these changes. In Chapter 5 we shall describe favorable aspects and costs of population growth. Chapter 6 will continue the subject of Chapter 5 and translate it into terms of optimum population size and distribution. In Chapter 7 we shall treat contrasts between growing and stationary populations (now in prospect in some countries), and then continue discussion of issues raised earlier.

I am indebted to the brotherhood of scholars for most of the contents. Some of them are identified in the short bibliography, but many remain anonymous. I am especially indebted to my wife Dorothy for her tolerance of floors littered for months with the multiplying contributions of this community and to my secretary, Mrs. Virginia Skinner, for getting the typescript into shape.

> Suppose that from floods, pestilences, failure
> of crops, or some such causes the race of men
> is reduced almost to extinction. Such things
> we are told have happened, and it is
> reasonable to think will happen again.
>
> POLYBIUS

This quotation from Polybius (a Greek historian during the second century before Christ) reveals some of the obstacles that impeded population growth until fairly modern times. It may also suggest why Polybius believed that "the true test of a perfect man is the power of bearing with spirit and dignity violent changes of fortune," or why Zeus declared, so Homer reported, that there is nothing "more piteous than a man, of all the things that creep and breathe upon the earth." Nor did conditions change dramatically during the next two millennia, when, as Fourastié put it, death was at the center of life and the churchyard at the center of the village. The chance of a newborn child's surviving to a given age, say five, twenty-one, or seventy, had not changed notably since Roman times, nor did numbers grow very much. The population of Europe—and of the world—was only about twice as large when Columbus discovered America as it was in the days of Christ and Caesar Augustus.

1.1. STABLE POPULATION

CHAPTER ONE

We can understand Polybius, Plato, and others better if we use a stable population model, one

Population Growth: Past and Prospective

whose age and sex composition are constant (that is, the sex ratio and the fraction of any age group in the total population, say those under 30, don't change). A stable population that is stationary corresponds to a life-table population: it will diminish in size if the assumed death rates give rise to more deaths than do the assumed birth rates, and it will increase if births exceed deaths.

A stable population is a theoretical construct. It is often approximated in the world of reality, but it is seldom matched completely or for long. It comes into being only when mortality, natality, and the sex ratio are stable for a long enough period of time. By mortality we mean the pattern of age-specific death rates, the deaths per year per 1000 persons in each single-year (that is, nineteenth year of life) or five-year (15 to 19 years) age group. By natality we mean the pattern of age-specific fertility rates, the births per year per 1000 women of child-bearing age in each single year (that is, twenty-second year of life) or five-year (20 to 24 years) age group.

In Table 1-1 I present in summary form the leading characteristics of the kinds of stable population that might have developed before the nineteenth century, when mortality was high and the expectation of life at birth was generally under 40 years. I have generated the values in this table by combining mortality and fertility patterns, and have supposed three expectations of life at birth (E)—20, 30 and 40 years—to represent mortality. By expectation of life at birth we mean the *average* number of years a person will live. For example, let's start with a cohort of 10,000 live-born females; some will die soon after birth, many will die before they are 20, and a few will live to 50 and beyond. If the whole cohort accumulates 300,000 years of life, 30 is the *average* to which members of the cohort may look forward; some will live fewer than 30 years, some will live more.

The fertility pattern we assume is represented by the Gross Reproduction Rate (*G.R.R.*), which is the average number of female births a member of a cohort of 1000 newly born females would have if no female died before she completed the childbearing period, which ranges (say) from the thirteenth to the fiftieth years. If the *G.R.R.* is 4.0 the cohort will produce 4000 female and about 4200 male births, or slightly over 8000 births; if the *G.R.R.* is 2.0, the number is cut in half.[1]

The crude birth and death rates in Table 1-1—*B.R.* and *D.R.*—are products of the age composition and the mortality and fertility associated with the assumed life expectancies and Gross Reproduction Rates; they

[1] The *G.R.R.* is, of course, a suppositious index, because even today in the United States only about 978 of 1000 newly born white females attain the thirteenth year, and only about 928 reach the fiftieth.

Table 1-1

High-Mortality Stable Population

G.R.R.	E=20					E=30					E=40				
	P.	A.	B.R.	D.R.	N.I.	P.	A.	B.R.	D.R.	N.I.	P.	A.	B.R.	D.R.	N.I.
4.0	52.4	2.4	63.8	53.0	10.8	49.2	2.6	59.8	35.3	24.5	47.3	2.7	57.3	24.1	33.2
3.0	57.6	3.9	50.5	50.2	0.3	54.5	4.1	47.7	33.7	14.0	52.5	4.4	46.0	23.3	22.7
2.5	60.7	5.2	42.8	49.1	-6.3	57.6	5.5	40.6	33.2	7.4	55.6	5.9	39.3	23.2	16.1
2.0	64.0	7.1	34.2	48.6	-14.4	60.9	7.7	32.7	33.6	-0.9	58.8	8.3	31.7	23.7	8.0
1.5	66.9	10.5	24.8	49.7	-24.9	63.8	11.5	23.8	35.0	-11.2	61.6	12.5	23.1	25.6	-2.5
1.0	68.3	16.9	14.6	54.4	-39.8	65.0	18.7	14.0	39.9	-25.9	62.6	20.4	13.6	30.9	-17.3

Source: The Aging of Populations and Its Economic and Social Implications *(New York: United Nations, 1956), p. 27.*
Abbreviations: G.R.R.: Gross Reproduction Rate; E: Expectation of life at birth; P: Percentage of stable population aged 15–59; A: Percentage of stable population aged 60 and over; B.R.: Births per 1000 inhabitants; D.R.: Deaths per 1000 inhabitants; N.I.: Excess of births over deaths per 1000 inhabitants

indicate the numbers of births and deaths per 1000 inhabitants; the difference between the two is the crude rate of natural increase. Table 1-2 presents a low-mortality stable population in keeping with modern times.

Table 1-1 provides a variety of information, three aspects of which are relevant here. First, a *G.R.R.* of 3.0 will just about balance deaths given a life expectancy of 20, but it enables a population to increase 1.4 percent per year if life expectancy is 30 years. Given a life expectancy of 27.5 years in a stable female population, a *G.R.R.* of about 2.5 yielding a birth rate of about 38 is required to balance mortality, according to tables prepared by Coale and Demeny; a slightly higher *G.R.R.* will allow some population growth.[2] Second, *P*, the percentage of population of productive age—those aged 15 to 59—is much higher than in many underdeveloped countries, where only around half the people are 15 to 59. Third, high mortality and low natality both reduce the percentage of persons under 15, for, given a *G.R.R.* of 3, this percentage is 43.1 when *E* equals 40 but only 38.5 when *E* equals 20.

Table 1-1 suggests that under what may be called normal conditions some population growth is to be expected, even given high mortality. For example, even so low a rate of population growth as one-fourth of one percent per year will increase a population about 28 percent per century and cause it to grow about 2.5 times every five centuries. According to our standards man's numbers long grew with extraordinary slowness, so increase must have been checked periodically. We presume it was held down by adverse events such as crop failures, epidemics, sickly seasons, and wars (which sometimes also spread epidemic disease and intensified shortage of subsistence). Food shortages due to crop failures were not easy to alleviate or guard against, because food output did not often greatly exceed requirements, storage facilities were inefficient, means of transportation were inadequate, and communications were poor. Epidemics in particular could wipe out accumulated growth. Most striking was the effect of the Black Death in Europe. Europe grew from about 50 million in 1150 to 73 million by 1300, declined to 51 million by 1350 and 45 million by 1400, and did not return to the 1300 level until around 1520. It was partly because numbers grew so slowly (when they grew at all) that moralists and political writers commonly enjoined man to increase and multiply.

When post-1800 conditions are contrasted with those obtaining earlier and those reflected in Table 1-1, several implications stand out, mainly consequences of increase in life expectancy. These are also implicit in

---

[2] Bibliographical data about works cited in the text by name of author or authors may be found in the bibliography at the end of the book.

Table 1-2

Low-Mortality Stable Population

G.R.R.	E=50					E=60.4					E=70.2				
	P.	A.	B.R.	D.R.	N.I.	P.	A.	B.R.	D.R.	N.I.	P.	A.	B.R.	D.R.	N.I.
4.0	45.8	2.7	55.7	16.2	39.5	44.4	2.7	54.1	9.4	44.7	43.3	2.6	52.7	4.1	48.6
3.0	50.9	4.5	44.9	15.8	29.1	49.6	4.4	43.8	9.6	34.2	48.4	4.3	42.9	4.8	38.1
2.5	53.9	6.1	38.4	16.0	22.4	52.6	6.0	37.7	10.1	27.6	51.4	5.9	37.0	5.5	31.5
2.0	57.2	8.6	31.1	16.8	14.3	55.8	8.6	30.6	11.1	19.5	54.7	8.5	30.1	6.8	23.3
1.5	60.0	13.0	22.7	18.8	3.9	58.7	13.1	22.5	13.5	9.0	57.7	13.0	22.3	9.4	12.9
1.0	60.7	21.5	13.4	24.3	-10.9	59.4	21.9	13.3	19.0	-5.7	58.6	21.9	13.3	15.1	-1.8

Source and abbreviations: Same as in Table 1-1

the life expectancy figures in Table 1-2, which roughly fit the circumstances at the close of the nineteenth century and thereafter. Life expectancy at birth in Norway did not move above 50 even for females until in the 1870s, or in Sweden until in the 1880s; with very few exceptions it did not reach 50 in most countries, including the United States, until the twentieth century. In the eighteenth century the average length of life in civilized localities was probably 35 to 40 years. It may occasionally have been this high before 1700 and in the Iberian and African portions of the Roman Empire, but it was relatively lower in urban and less favored areas in and after Roman times. It may have been as high as 30 in ancient Greece, but it was lower in prehistoric times. Today, therefore, women with a life expectancy of 75 or more are living at least twice as long as their ancestors two centuries ago and two and one-half to three times as long as their counterparts in ancient times.

Increase in life expectancy has put pressure on man to reduce fertility. For example, suppose the *G.R.R.* is in the neighborhood of 2.5. If life expectancy were around 30, deaths would roughly balance births, and the ratio of children under 15 to persons 15 to 59 would be 36.9/57.6, or 0.64. If, however, a life expectancy of 60.4 is combined with a *G.R.R.* of 2.5, natural increase will approximate 2.7 percent and the ratio of persons under 15 to those aged 15 to 59 will rise to 41.4/52.6, or 0.79. In either situation only about six persons in 100 would be 60 or more. Pressure of dependents on adults and resources and facilities might then tend to reduce the value attached to children.

1.2. POPULATION GROWTH

Information relating to population growth and distribution has until recently been so spotty that estimates of numbers are quite conjectural. We only pretend to have relatively firm estimates for the period since the mid-seventeenth century. Near the beginning of the Christian era the world's population was probably between 200 and 250 million. This number is far larger than the 5 million estimated for the Mesolithic cultural stage 8000 years earlier, by which time, E. S. Deevy calculates, some 30 billion hunters and gatherers may have lived and died. The great increase between Mesolithic times and the beginnings of the Christian era was mainly the result of the agricultural revolution, which partially removed restraints upon population growth and made possible village farming and urban living. This revolution increased man's numbers by a factor of something like 16 between 8000 and 4000 B.C. and by a further factor of about two and one-half between 4000 B.C. and the advent of the Christian era, given populations at these two points in time of 87 and 225 million. Of the world's estimated 200 to 250 million at the beginning of the Christian era, about three-fifths lived in Asia, mainly in China and India, which along with the Roman Empire accounted for about four-fifths of the world's population. Europe's share probably fell short of one-seventh, and Africa's was slightly smaller than Europe's.

The majority of the world's population has continued to live in Asia, though this majority has been reduced by the growth of population in the Americas and Africa, which, M. K. Bennett estimates, numbered 28 million and 67 million respectively in 1300. Europe's population, held down by the collapse of the Roman Empire and its aftermath, flourished after 1000, so that by 1300 it numbered about 73 million, compared with 34 million in 30 A.D.; at the same time Asia had 216 million, compared with about 138 million in 30 A.D. Europe's population was reduced perhaps 37 percent by plague and associated disturbances, but by 1650 it had increased to about 100 million, Asia's to 320 to 330 million. Europe's share remained just below one-fifth, about what it had been in 1300, whereas Asia's increased to about three-fifths, compared with about five-ninths in 1300. Africa's population apparently had ceased to grow by 1650; it numbered then 90 to 100 million, or about one-sixth of the world's population. America's population probably numbered not much more than 10 million, compared with a peak of 40 million or more at the time of Columbus. Around 1950 Europe's share of the world's population was about 23 percent, Asia's about 55 percent, Africa's about 8 percent, and that of the Americas about 13 percent. In summary, between the opening of the Christian era and around 1950 Europe's share of the world's population increased, Asia's declined, Africa's declined greatly, and that of the Americas increased remarkably, though not so notably when compared with their share in 1500, around 9 percent.

The estimates in Table 1-3 indicate that the rate of population growth has increased over time. In Asia the annual rate rose from about five-twelfths of one percent during the period 1650 to 1900 to around two-thirds of one percent during the war- and depression-ridden period 1900 to 1950, and then to 1.9 percent during the period 1950 to 1965. Europe's annual rate rose from about five-twelfths of one percent during the 1650–1800 period through nearly three-fourths of one percent in the 1800–1900 period, fell to two-thirds of one percent in 1900–1950, then rose to slightly over one percent during the 1950–1965 period. Africa's population, slightly smaller in 1850 than in 1650, increased about one-third of one percent per year during 1850–1900 and about one percent per year in 1900–1950; its growth had accelerated to around 2.1 percent per year by 1950–1965. Latin America's rate of 2.85 percent during the

Table 1-3

Estimated Population, by Continent, 1650–1950 (in millions)

Region	1650	1800	1850	1900	1950
Africa	100	90	95	120	199
Asia (excl. U.S.S.R.)	327	597	741	915	1272
Europe (incl. U.S.S.R.)	103	192	274	423	594
Latin America	12	19	33	63	162
Northern America	1	6	26	81	166
Oceania	2	2	2	6	13
World Total	545	906	1171	1608	2406

Source: The Determinants and Consequences of Population Trends *(New York: United Nations, 1953), p. 11.*

period 1950 to 1965 exceeded both the 1900–1950 rate of 1.87 percent and the nineteenth-century rate of about 2.37 percent. Only Northern America grew more rapidly during the nineteenth century (about 2.6 percent per year) than during the 1900–1950 period (1.4 percent) or the 1950–1965 period (1.7 percent). The growth rate of the world's population rose from about five-twelfths of one percent during the 1650–1800 period to close to one percent during the nineteenth century. It fell to slightly below seven-eighths of one percent in 1900–1950, then it rose to 1.8 percent in 1950–1965.

From the standpoint of the increase in pressure upon a finite environment, the absolute growth rate may be more relevant. In the 1850s about 68 million were added to the world's population; in 1900–1910, 90 million; and in 1950–1960, 482 million—seven times as many as in 1850–1960, three-fourths of them in the underdeveloped world. By the 1990s the figure could be 942 million, of whom about seven-eighths would be in underdeveloped regions. In short, people are being added to a finite world at a rate about seven times that of a century ago, and this rate could soon be double that of the 1950s.

1.3. MIGRATION

Although growth of the world population as a whole and in large countries is the result of an excess of births over deaths, the growth of smaller bodies of people—states, regions, cities—has been modified by migration, the most important form of which has been from rural areas to cities, long described as consumers of men (see Chapter 2). Here we are concerned with intercountry migration (which is often also intercontinental migration).

Migration has tended to increase the rate of population growth in a number of ways. First, migrants either have carried superior methods of production to their new homes, have learned superior methods there, or have been shaken out of traditional, less productive ways and become more productive. The result has increased return in underpeopled regions of destination (for example, Australia and North America). Second, overall employment conditions have sometimes been improved, both at home and in countries of destination. The net effect of these movements has been to increase the total output of goods and services, and this has tended to make natural increase higher than it otherwise would have been. This must also have been true, to a lesser extent, of earlier migrations, such as those that spread numbers over medieval Europe, or the ones reported by Thucydides that relieved local population pressure in Hellas.

The contribution of international migration to world population is not really determinable other than on arbitrary assumptions about the behavior of returns and the response of natural increase, but the major share is imputable to intercontinental migration, mainly from Europe to the Western Hemisphere, principally the United States. Before 1800 net immigration from Europe to America north of the Rio Grande approximated 2 million, a total perhaps 20 times higher than that into Latin America. Later, with improvements in transportation and the establishment of relatively stable governments in the New World, emigration from Europe increased. Woytinsky puts the number settling permanently in the United States and Canada between 1600 and the 1930s at more than 25 million, and those settling permanently in the Middle and South Americas at close to 18 million. A much smaller number settled in Africa and Oceania. Whether this outflow retarded European population growth depends on whether natural increase in Europe was stimulated enough to offset the outflow in the longer run, in part as a result of the expansion of markets and sources of produce abroad.

Of the approximately 20 million Africans taken from their homes and sold as slaves after the discovery of America, nearly 15 million of them were sent to the Western Hemisphere, about a million of these to the United States where, between 1790 and 1870, the high natality of the Negro population increased its number about 2.5 percent per year despite high mortality. Most of the other slaves removed from Africa were sent to the Caribbean region and Latin America, where they contributed importantly to the racial composition of the population.

Emigration from Asia to other continents was much smaller than voluntary emigration from Europe and forced emigration from Africa, in part because emigrants from Asia were not freely admitted into the

Western Hemisphere or Oceania, but were introduced as a rule as indentured laborers. Emigration from Asia may have stimulated population growth in some countries of origin by relieving the pressure of numbers on arable land, but it did not stimulate such growth appreciably because of the predominance of males among those who moved abroad. South and East Asia contributed most of Asia's emigrants. As of 1940, according to a United Nations study, about 8.5 million Chinese lived outside of China, of whom only 300 to 400 thousand lived outside Asia. About 30 million emigrants, mostly male, left British India between 1834 and 1937, but of these about 24 million returned. As of the late 1940s about 4 million Indians lived outside India and Pakistan, mainly in Asia and Africa. Most of the 3.5 million Japanese civilians living outside Japan in 1940 were in the Far East; hence many were repatriated after World War II. The 2.8 million Koreans living abroad in 1940, representing about one-eighth of Korea's population, resided mainly in Manchuria and Japan.

1.4. MORTALITY, NATALITY, AND NATURAL INCREASE

The rate of population growth in the underdeveloped world began to pull away from that in the developed world in the depression-ridden 1930s. The annual rates of increase per decade in the developed and underdeveloped regions, respectively, were 0.87 and 0.36 percent in 1900–1910, 1.17 and 0.41 in 1910–1920, and 0.8 and 1.18 in 1920–1930. Not even the residue of the baby boom in the 1950s eliminated this difference, since the rate in the underdeveloped world rose to 2.01 percent while that in the developed world increased only to 1.3 percent. Over the four decades from 1960 to 2000, as we have already implied, population in the underdeveloped world is expected to grow about twice as fast as that in the developed world, probably somewhat over 2.1 percent as compared with 1.0 percent. A rapid decline in mortality in the underdeveloped world, coupled with little change in natality, has been responsible for this difference in rates of growth, whereas in the developed world both natality and mortality declined, thus continuing, with some acceleration, trends under way in the nineteenth century. Even more important have been the ways in which fertility- and mortality-governing forces have operated. In developed countries the forces that produced a very gradual decline in mortality operated in direct conjunction with related forces to set in motion a slow decline in natality, but in underdeveloped countries the forces at work were exogenous. Death control, introduced from abroad in the present century, met with little resistance, since most people prefer life to death. Birth control was not introduced at the time death control came in, nor was there effort to introduce it after the need became apparent; too many social and other obstacles stood in the way.

The decline in natality in today's advanced countries began, in most instances, in the nineteenth century, but it was manifest from the start only in France and in the native white population of the United States. The levels of natality from which the decline began were lower in Western Europe than those in today's underdeveloped world, where the number of births per 1000 ranges from about 40 to 54 and the Gross Reproduction Rate from about 2.7 to 3.4 In Eastern Europe and Russia, however, the levels were higher than in the West, and in most of those countries they long remained comparable to those in today's high-fertility countries, with births numbering 40 to 45 per 1000 inhabitants. The birth rate for Europe as a whole, about 39 per 1000 persons in the early nineteenth century, had fallen only to about 35 by 1880, declining less than half a point per decade; the Gross Reproduction Rate was still at or slightly above 2.0, down only about a fifth from what it had been in the early nineteenth century.

Western birth rates were already diverging appreciably even before 1880. At this time in Eastern Europe the rate ranged from over 40 to nearly 50, while in Northern and Western Europe it was about 33; in Central and Southern Europe rates fell between these extremes, generally centering around 35.

The period from 1900 to 1950, with two world wars and a great depression, witnessed an irregular but generally downward trend in natality. The birth rate in Northern and Western Europe descended from about 33 in 1876–1880 to 24 by 1911–1914, to 19 by 1925–1929, and to a low of 16 in 1935–1939, after which it rose temporarily to 20 in 1945–1954, only to fall back to 18 in 1955–1959. The birth rates in Central Europe were around or below 35 on the eve of World War I, but fell to 23 by the late 1920s and to 19 by 1955–1959. Those in Southern Europe were also around or below 35 at the beginning of World War I, but they fell to 31 by the late 1920s and to 21 by 1955–1959. Birth rates in Eastern Europe ranged from 34 to 40 in the early 1920s but declined to 19 to 25 by 1955–1959, while those in Russia fell from around 43 in 1926–1927 to 30 in the early 1930s, rose in the late 1930s only to be depressed by war, and subsequently moved in the 1950s from about 27 to 25. Upsurges in natality after 1918, in the late 1930s, and after 1945 did little more than compensate in some measure for birth deficits associated with war and depression.

Even though natality was generally late to decline in Europe and then declined slowly until after World War I, the rate of natural increase was low. In Western Europe this was because of the low level of natality even before the decline set in and because of the slowness with which mortality declined. The population of the whole of Europe including the Soviet Union increased not quite three-fourths of one percent per year in 1800–1850 and only about seven-eighths of one percent per year in 1850–1900, but even this was above the five-twelfths of one percent of Asia, where high mortality largely offset high natality. Europe's growth rate might have been higher had there been no emigration, given that emigration did not stimulate natural increase in Europe. In Western Europe the rate of natural increase was below or not much above 1.0 percent. Even in Eastern Europe before World War I the rate of natural increase was in the neighborhood of 1.5 percent or lower; there too high mortality partly balanced high natality. Natural increase declined after the baby boom of the late 1940s, until in the 1950s it was lower than in 1910–1913 but not so low as in the late 1930s.

The rate of natural increase was held down in nineteenth-century Europe (though not in the post-1920 underdeveloped world) partly because mortality fell slowly in the former and rapidly in the latter. Several contrasts serve to illustrate the difference. Consider data covering a period of 38 to 48 years. Decline per decade in deaths per 1000 inhabitants ranged from 3.1 in Egypt to 4.3 in Taiwan and 4.5 in Ceylon. Corresponding rates of decline in Western European countries ranged roughly from about one per decade in France to about two in Austria and the Netherlands. The rate of decline has been at least twice as fast in the underdeveloped countries during this century. This conclusion is supported by a comparison of increases in expectation of life at birth. An increase in male life expectancy from around 40 to 60 took over 80 years in England, Denmark, and France; it rose about 2.2 years per decade. But in Chile, Taiwan, Jamaica, Ceylon, and Mexico male life expectancy moved from 32–41 to 50–66 years, a rise of 6.6 and 8.4 years per decade. The rate of increase in these underdeveloped countries thus was about three times as fast as that in Western Europe. This is consistent with the apparent rule that in countries where natality and mortality are late to decline the rate of decline is relatively high once decline sets in.

1.5. THE FUTURE

The United Nations has attempted a number of projections based on different assumptions. Such projections are subject to considerable uncertainty, even in the absence of devastating war (of which thermonuclear war is most destructive). First, gross reproduction and natality may deviate temporarily from those projected, if only because the timing and pattern of average family formation change. Second, mortality may be lower than anticipated, particularly when expectation of life is low by current standards, as is true of a number of underdeveloped countries. These and other uncertainties compel projectors to develop a number of projections based on a variety of assumptions regarding the future behavior of natality and mortality. Table 1-4 summarizes the medium United Nations projection based on an assessment of world population prospects as of 1970.

The rates of increase, the percentages in the fourth column, indicate that differential growth is greatly modifying the distribution of the world's population. Furthermore, changes in distribution will continue into the twenty-first century along much the same lines, should the rates of growth expected for 1990–2000 and reported in the next-to-last column be approximated. The proportion of the world's population situated in the less developed countries will rise from 67.3 percent in 1960 to 76.1 percent in 2000; between 1900 and 1920, when mortality was very high in underdeveloped countries, this proportion fell from 66.7 percent to 63.8 percent. The percentage anticipated for the more developed regions in 2000, 32.7, will approximate that in 1900, 33.3.

Of the 3.5 billion increase in world population expected in 1960–2000, about 4 percent are anticipated in regions of high density (136 to 252 persons per square kilometer), 58 percent in regions of moderate density (46 to 98 persons per square kilometer), and 38 percent in regions of low density (2 to 20 persons per square kilometer). Within the under-developed world, it is anticipated, will be found one-twentieth of the increase expected in regions of moderate density, about four-ninths of that expected in regions of high density, and nearly four-fifths of that expected in regions of low density. The most important effects of per-sisting population growth in the underdeveloped world, as we shall show in Chapters 3 and 4, will be increase in (a) the relative number of persons in regions with inadequate amounts of arable land or physical capital or both, and (b) the fraction of the world's population with a relatively high number of young dependents.

Let us turn now to the bases of the demographic conditions that underlie the projections in Table 1-4. These rest upon the assumption that in the developed world as a whole the crude birth rate will decline from 20 per 1000 inhabitants in the 1960s to 18 in the 1990s, and in the underdeveloped world from 41 in the 1960s (even as in 1900 and 1940) to 29 in the 1990s. Meanwhile the crude death rate will rise from 9 to 10 in the developed world and decline from 17 to 8 in the underdeveloped world, whence the rate of natural increase will decline from 11 to 8 per

Table 1-4

Growth of Population, World and Regional, 1960–2000

Region	Population (millions)		Increase in percent		Persons per km² in 1960
	1960	2000	1960–2000	1990–2000	
(0) World Total	2986	6494	117	19.4	22
(1) More Developed Regions	976	1454	49	8.8	—
(2) Europe	425	568	34	6.6	86
(3) U.S.S.R.	214	330	54	9.2	10
(4) Northern America	199	333	67	11.0	9
(5) Japan	93	133	43	6.4	252
(6) Temperate South America	33	63	91	14.5	8
(7) Australia and New Zealand	13	26	100	15.4	2
(8) Less Developed Regions	2010	5040	151	22.9	—
(9) South Asia	865	2354	172	23.1	56
(10) East Asia (exc. 5)	692	1291	87	13.2	61
(11) Africa	270	818	203	33.3	9
(12) Latin America (exc. 6)	180	588	227	32.4	11
(13) Oceania (exc. 7)	3	9	200	31.9	5

Source: The World Population Situation in 1970 (*New York: United Nations, 1971*), p. 46.

1000 inhabitants in the developed world and from 24 to 21 in the under-developed world.

The figures in the preceding paragraph are averages for the developed and the underdeveloped worlds, respectively; both the crude birth rate and the crude death rate will continue to vary considerably from country to country in the underdeveloped world, much more so than in the developed world. As countries develop and are modernized, their birth rates converge, as do their death rates.

The future growth of the world's population depends mainly on what happens in the underdeveloped world, both because of its extent and because of the likelihood that decline in fertility will continue to be partly offset by decline in mortality. With a life expectancy at birth of 70 or more years in the developed world and a Gross Reproduction Rate of 1.3 or less, population in the developed world will grow not much more than 0.5 percent per year, if that. Meanwhile, even with a *G.R.R.* of 2.3, anticipated in the underdeveloped world by the 1980s, and a life expectancy of 58–60 years, its population will continue to grow 2 or more percent per year. Even if its *G.R.R.* should decline to between 1.5 and 1.75, its population could continue to grow between 1.0 and 1.5 percent per year, enough to double its numbers every 47–70 years. Indeed, with a life expectancy of 70 or more years population continues to grow until the *G.R.R.* approaches 1.0.

When the world's population will stop growing and what it will then number remain subject to guess. According to one estimate the world's population will number 11 billion in 2050, of which 9 billion will live in underdeveloped countries. If we assume that the population in the developed world is approximately stationary and that the Net Reproduction Rate in the underdeveloped world has just approximated 1.0, we may infer that the world's population will be nearly stationary by the year 2100, at something like 15 to 17 billion. Arable land per person would then be around one-half acre.

1.6. THE DEVELOPED VERSUS THE UNDERDEVELOPED WORLD

The countries of the world, classified in terms of fertility, fall into two distinct sets, those with high fertility and those with low fertility. In the low-fertility countries around 1960 Gross Reproduction Rates ranged from 1.2 to 1.8 and averaged 1.4; by 1965–1970 this average had fallen to 1.3 though the range remained unchanged. In high-fertility countries around 1960 Gross Reproduction Rates ranged from 2.2 to 3.4 and averaged about 2.7; in 1965–1970 the rates ranged from 2.1 to 3.2 and averaged 2.7, as they had in 1960. The average for the world as a whole, according to United Nations experts, approximated 2.3 in 1965–1970, as it had in 1960. By the 1980s the Gross Reproduction Rate could decline to 2.3 in the underdeveloped world, with rates by region ranging from 2.1 to 3.2. Then, with the rate at 1.3 in the developed world, the world rate would approximate 2.0; this rate, combined with a life expectancy of about 60 years, would permit a rate of population growth of about 2 percent per year.

Table 1-5 contrasts socioeconomic characteristics of high-fertility countries with those of low-fertility countries as of 1960. The values reported for the socioeconomic indicators were obtained by grouping those found in each set of countries into three categories, low, medium, and high.

Table 1-5

Fertility and Economic and Social Indicators

Indicators	Value of Indicators	
	Low Fertility	High Fertility
Gross Reproduction Rates	under 1.3-1.99	2.3-3.10 and over
Income per head	$308-$522	under $88-$307
Energy consumption per head	900-3300 and over	under 100-899
% of population in cities of 20,000 and over	27-45 and over	under 9-26
% of economically active males outside agriculture	55-85 and over	under 25-54
Hospital beds per 1000 inhabitants	2.5-10 and over	under 1.25-2.49
Expectation of life at birth (both sexes)	64.5-70.5 and over	under 50.5-64.4
Infant mortality	under 22-42	43-92 and over
% of women 15-19 married	under 3-7	8-33 and over
% of literates among females 15 and over	68-98 and over	under 14-67
Newspaper circulation per 1000 inhabitants	105-340 and over	under 10-104
Radio receivers per 1000 inhabitants	80-261 and over	under 7-79
Cinema attendance per person	8.3-14.3 and over	under 2.3-8.2

Source: Population Bulletin, No. 7 (New York: United Nations, 1963), Chap. 9.

Because these characteristics are intercorrelated it is not possible to determine with precision the degree to which variation in fertility is associated with variation in any one indicator. United Nations experts report that

high-fertility and low-fertility countries differ greatly in every aspect of economic and social advancement represented by the indicators, while within each

180711

of these groups, the differences in average values of the indicators according to particular levels of fertility are comparatively slight and often of doubtful statistical significance.

Apparently change in the value of our indicators exercises little if any influence on fertility until this value passes a "threshold" level, and even then the indicators differ greatly in their influence on fertility. Nonetheless, fertility tends to move downward, to enter a transition stage from high to low levels, as more and more indicators move beyond the "threshold" range of values. Careful analysis would show these indicators to be both economic and noneconomic in character.

Negotiating a transit from high fertility levels to low fertility levels could prove easier for today's underdeveloped countries than it was for present-day developed countries, some of which required over half a century to move from fairly high to low levels. The experience of a few small underdeveloped countries since 1950 suggests that the transition period may be declining, perhaps by one-half. Such a decline is not suggested, of course, by a superficial comparison of the demographic past of developed countries with the demographic present of most underdeveloped countries. For in most European countries (but not those in Eastern Europe) Gross Reproduction Rates were in the neighborhood of 2.5 or lower, from which levels they moved to present levels of around 1.3. By contrast, in the underdeveloped regions the Gross Reproduction Rate in 1965–1970 approximated 2.7, ranging, outside East Asia, from around 2.4 to 3.2, which implies birth rates of roughly 35 to 49 per 1000 population. Underdeveloped regions started from much higher levels, therefore, than did nineteenth-century Western countries. Nonetheless, there are offsetting conditions. Today contraceptive methods are far more advanced, often have the active endorsement of the state, and are strongly opposed by cults and ideological groups only in some countries. Moreover, high fertility combines with low infant and child mortality to impose a heavier dependency burden on adults than was the case in the West in the nineteenth century, when children required less education and entered the labor force earlier. Urbanization also feeds the revolutionary change in man's aspirations now under way in much of the world. It is possible, therefore, that the transit to low natality, mortality, and natural increase will be completed more rapidly in the underdeveloped world than it was in the West.

As yet this is hardly happening. Births per 1000 in the underdeveloped countries declined only from 42 to 40.6 between 1960–1965 and 1965–1970, whereas in the West they declined from 20.5 to 18.6. The crude death rate in 1937 ranged from 11 to 18 per 1000 inhabitants in the developed world and from 20 to 35 in the underdeveloped world, but it declined nearly everywhere in the 1940s and 1950s. Between the late 1950s and early 1970s, however, this rate remained virtually unchanged (at around 9) in the developed world, whereas in the underdeveloped world it declined from 22 in the 1950s to 17 in the 1960s. Accordingly, natural increase rose to 24 per 1000 in the underdeveloped world in the 1960s while declining to 11 in the developed world. Since life expectancy at birth in the developed world averages 71 years, it cannot increase notably there, but it can increase greatly in the underdeveloped world: in the late 1960s it ranged from 39 in Middle Africa to 60 in Latin America.

1.7. THE PATH TO ZERO RATE OF POPULATION GROWTH

Population must in time cease to grow, either because man controls his growth or because it is controlled for him by the finitude of his physical environment and the elements that enter into his standard of life. The present likelihood that population growth will soon come to a halt in the absence of thermonuclear war is remote. It is true that the United Nations medium projection made in 1963 postulated a decline of three points per decade in natality—from 40.4 to 28—between 1960 and 2000 and that if this decline were to continue until near the middle of the twenty-first century natality would be at a level (say 14) corresponding to the true death rate in the stationary population with a life expectancy of about 70 years. When such a stationary population finally came into existence, the Gross Reproduction Rate would be slightly above 1.0, and birth and death rates would both be in the neighborhood of 14, given a life expectancy for the two sexes in the neighborhood of 70. It is by no means certain, however, that the decline in natality currently postulated and actually under way in some underdeveloped countries will continue until a stationary demographic state is realized. Indeed, according to the United Nations 1970 projection, the world rate of natural increase will decline very little between 1960 and 2000.

Movement to a zero rate of population growth consists of two stages: (1) movement to a replacement level at which the Net Reproduction Rate (*N.R.R.*) approximates 1.0 and current age-specific mortality and fertility rates would show as many deaths as births were the actual population stable and stationary in age composition; and (2) adjustment of the age composition of the actual population to that of a stable stationary population—wherein deaths equal births and the birth rate equals the death rate in a range somewhere between 13 and 15 per 1,000 inhabitants. Movement from completion of stage (1) to completion of stage

(2) will take roughly 60 to 65 years, during which, according to a U.S. Bureau of the Census study, the population will increase another 50 to 85 percent.

The case of India may be used to illustrate the cost of delay in completing stage (1) and reducing the N.R.R. to 1.0, the replacement level. In 1970 India had a population of 576 million and an N.R.R. of 2.091, sufficient to increase its population over forty-fold in a century. Should India reduce its N.R.R. to 1.0 by the early 1980s, its population would level off at 1211 million by 2045. But were it to delay reducing the N.R.R. to 1.0 until 2000 to 2005, its population would not level off until 2060, and then at 1763 millions. The delay of twenty years would have increased the population by 45 percent.

Presumably, the pressure that India's population will be under as a result of shortage of land and employment opportunities will eventuate in a reduction of the N.R.R. to 1.0. Until now, however, response to actual or prospective pressure has not been great in India or in many other high-fertility countries in Asia, Africa, and Latin America.

1.8. FERTILITY AND ENVIRONMENTAL SCARCITY

The contents of the previous section recall man's experience prior to the eighteenth century, which showed that if numbers are not checked then environmental limitations will constrain growth, through mortality if not through control of fertility. Before about 1700 Western Europe's economy was quasi-stationary. Population growth between 1000 and 1750 averaged about 17 percent per century, Kuznets estimates, and increase of average output was at an even lower rate, not much in excess of 10 percent per century in countries experiencing income growth.

The limitations to growth before 1700 were essentially physical-environmental, for increase in output was associated almost completely with increase in inputs of physical capital and labor. After 1700 a new type of economy emerged, the precise nature of which was not recognized by nineteenth-century economists, such as David Ricardo and John Stuart Mill, who anticipated the advent of a stationary state in which the rate of return on capital would just suffice to keep its stock intact and the level of wages would just suffice to induce population replacement. Underlying this stationary economy were physical-environmental limitations to which man could respond, as he had in the past, by controlling his numbers or experiencing rising mortality. Growth in eighteenth-century England (from 1695 to 1785) somewhat supports such expectations, since according to Kuznets's estimates numbers grew about 30 percent and average output about 20 percent.

After 1800, however, the growth process changed. In 1801–1871 the rate of population growth in England approximated 270 percent per century, and that of average output 230 percent per century. Thereafter the rate of population growth fell while that of average output rose. In time, increase in the input of labor and physical capital came to account for only about 20 to 25 percent of the increase in output, compared with nearly 100 percent before 1700; improvements in labor and capital, together with investment in such improvements, accounted for the balance. (Of course when costs other than those of labor and capital are taken into account, the net rate of growth per capita is reduced by about one-tenth or more.)

The change in the nature of the growth process has modified the nature of the relationship between physical-environmental limitations and the pressure on man to limit his numbers. Before 1700 and even until the early nineteenth century the physical environment set limits to the rate at which important items (e.g., food) could be satisfied within the budgets of households and thus prompted control of numbers (e.g., through deferment of marriage, and neglect of infants and very young children). Under modern conditions in advanced countries, physical-environmental limits operate not at all or very little through limitation of food and raw material supplies; instead they operate through constraints on the availability per capita of those elements in the physical environment which play an important part in the living standards of persons residing in high-income countries. Illustrative are natural amenities based upon the physical environment, the relative prices of which will continue to rise.

In sum, as numbers grow components of the environment become scarce and rise in relative price. How many children a couple decides to have is affected by these price changes as well as by other factors. Environmental scarcity, when it emerges, always influences fertility, but in ways that change, in ways quite different today from what they were before 1700. Such scarcity can, therefore, eventuate in a zero rate of population growth, though one quite differently grounded than the near-zero rate of growth prior to, say, 1700.

> This, then, is the conclusion of the city's
> history; growing from primitive barter-center
> to Culture-city and at last to world city,
> it...moves on to final self-destruction.
>
> OSWALD SPENGLER

While the spread of population over the world has been dominated by natural increase, the pattern within "states" has been greatly determined by economic and political conditions, especially the former. Internal migration has been the preponderant form of migration, mainly movement from the countryside, usually a source of population surplus, to the city, long known as a "consumer" of men because deaths often exceeded births. International migration complemented the distributive role of internal migration.

A distributive pattern could not develop until the more or less autonomous bands and villages men lived in were arranged into large autonomous political units under centralized government. The origins of this process, which got under way after 5000 B.C., have been variously explained by citing diverse "causative" forces. Carneiro, in his ecological theory of the origin of the state, suggests that increase in population density beyond a level critical for a particular environment played a part. Population growth may therefore be said to have contributed to the patterning of population distribution in the distant past as well as in modern times (in

CHAPTER TWO

Population Distribution: Past and Prospective

21

the sense that it made certain patterns possible, not that it determined which would emerge). Today it is far more possible to establish collective control over population distribution, as we shall show in Section 4 of this chapter, entitled "Regulatory Forces."

2.1. ECONOMIC DEVELOPMENT

The pattern of population distribution within an essentially autonomous state, though susceptible of variation, is subject to technological, physical, and other limits (see Section 2.3). The constraining influence of these limits has been reduced, of course, by increase in man's control over his physical environment.

Economic development has probably not been going on together with population concentration for longer than two centuries, if that long. It may be useful, therefore, to examine the process of economic development in its broad outlines, together with its relation to population concentration, especially to city growth, its major form.

Economic development consists of four interrelated movements.

1. Output—both agricultural produce and nonagricultural goods and services—and aggregate income must increase faster than the population. Growth of per capita income in the rural sector long tends to lag behind that in the urban sector, often even manifesting little tendency to rise at first, but finally it approaches the urban level. Eventually the rural sector must meet the competition of a relatively labor-short urban sector, competition that becomes more effective as the unemployed or underemployed members of the rural "labor force" are drawn into the urban sector. Shrinkage of the spread between rural and urban levels proceeds so irregularly, however, that it often is hard to see in the behavior of income and wage statistics, affected as they are by war, the trade cycle, and, in some countries (for example the United States), immigration of workers from abroad. Immigration decelerates the rise of wages outside more than inside the rural sector, which tends to slow down outmigration from the rural sector.

While major migratory trends may be incorporated into empirically acceptable and analytically explanatory models, the precise conditions to which particular potential migrants respond and how and why they respond as they do are ascertainable only through detailed local inquiry. Fortunately economic historians are now examining the operation of mechanisms affecting migration during the past several centuries.

2. Increase in average output and income presupposes the eventual engagement of a large fraction of a nation's gainfully employed population in industry and other nonagricultural activities. For, whereas the

aggregate demand for nonagricultural output keeps pace with aggregate income, the demand for agricultural produce finally grows little more rapidly than the total population. In other words, the income elasticity of demand per capita for nonagricultural output (the annual percentage increase in average income divided into the resulting percentage increase in rate of expenditure per capita on some category of aggregate output) often approximates or exceeds 1.0, while that for agricultural output is less than 1.0 unless average income is very low. Even should the latter approximate 1.0, it will decline as average income rises, perhaps to a lovel as low as 0.1 or less. The rate of growth of aggregate demand for any category of goods, D', grows roughly as does P' plus ey', where P' denotes the growth rate of aggregate population, y' denotes the rate of increase of average income y, and e designates income elasticity of individual demand for the category of goods in question. Suppose that the value of e is 1.0 for nonagricultural output and 0.5 for agricultural produce. Then if both P and y are growing one percent per year, D will grow about 2 percent per year for nonagricultural output and 1.5 percent per year for farm produce. Under these conditions, if agricultural output should continue to grow 2 percent per year, unemployment will tend to develop in the countryside unless outmigration reduces the agricultural population. Fertility too will tend to decline as the agricultural prospect becomes less attractive, but such a decline cannot cushion the pressure of increasing unemployment until 10 to 15 or more years later.

3. Output per agriculturalist and yield per acre must increase. If output per agriculturalist does not increase and population grows, the fraction of the labor force engaged in agriculture cannot decline and the absolute number so engaged must increase at least as fast as the total population and labor force. Moreover, in the absence of increase in yield per acre and per agriculturalist, the arable portion of a country's land area is finally brought under cultivation. Thereafter, the total population cannot long continue to increase, unless foreign sources can be drawn on for additional agricultural edibles and nonedibles (tobacco, cotton, and so forth). Increase in yield per acre defers the day when agricultural imports become essential. In practice, of course, increase in output per agriculturalist usually is accompanied by increase in yield per acre, though in theory an agriculturalist could increase his total output merely by tending more acres; the changes that increase output per agriculturalist tend also to increase yield per acre.

4. As we have implied, increases in both output per agriculturalist and yield per acre soon entail modernization of agriculture, and modernization calls for increased use of inputs—fertilizer, water, equipment that permits faster and better cultivation, pesticides and herbicides to control

competitors of plants and sources of animal ills, heightened agricultural skills, cultivation sequences that permit multiple cropping, transportation, and other ancillaries to agricultural activities—as partial substitutes for land and labor. Satisfactory marketing opportunities and price-cost relationships that make agricultural improvements sufficiently profitable are also essential.

The availability of these inputs and conditions depends in part on the degree to which the nonagricultural branches of an economy are modernized. Except partially with respect to death control, it is not generally possible to modernize one sector of an underdeveloped economy without also modernizing all or most of the other sectors, because sectors are interrelated by flow of income, output, inputs, technological skill, and applicable technical solutions. In summary, agricultural progress is essential but of limited applicability unless it is complemented by other forms of progress and control of population. It is because of the interrelatedness of economic components and the role of noneconomic cultural factors that modernization of agriculture and marked increase in output per agriculturalist and acre cannot be achieved in isolation. Traditional agriculture must be transformed into modern agriculture, with its different structures and procedures.

2.2. ECONOMIC DEVELOPMENT AND POPULATION PATTERNING

Economic development contributes to the distribution of a country's population (1) by generating a population surplus within the countryside and setting in motion a drift to the city, and (2) by changing modes of production in ways that confer advantages on some centers and regions.

In Section 2.1 we showed how labor surpluses emerge in the agricultural sector and the countryside because of limitations on the demand for agricultural produce in an economically progressive world. Without sufficiently expanding foreign markets for produce or enough emigration to foreign lands, these surpluses must seek employment and support in nonagricultural sectors of the economy. Emigration abroad may cushion the need to transfer to the nonagricultural sector (as it did in Europe before World War I), but it cannot eliminate it. Moreover, dividing agricultural output up according to conventional, communal rules instead of in keeping with the principle of reward according to productivity can do little more than cushion the pressure to move out of agriculture. Of course, given reward according to productivity, real wages would soon be pressed sufficiently below the level realizable outside agriculture to make it worthwhile for many to leave agricultural employment for other kinds of activity. Furthermore, when a country is in the process of settlement, those dissatisfied with the rewards of agriculture in particular areas may attempt to pursue them elsewhere (the westward movement in the United States that persisted until around the close of the nineteenth century is a case in point); this type of response slows down but does not stop the drift to town and city.

Should these qualifying circumstances described in Section 2.1 not be present, the agricultural sector tends to develop a surplus of labor under pressure to seek employment elsewhere. This pressure does not arise, of course, until output per agriculturalist begins to rise more rapidly than aggregate demand for agricultural produce. At times, especially in countries where agriculture is undergoing modernization, output per agriculturalist rises as rapidly as (if not more rapidly than) output per member of the nonagricultural labor force. In the preceding section we assumed an annual increase of one percent in both population and average output—that is, a 2 percent annual increase in potential income. This assumption also implied a 2 percent annual increase in total agricultural output, given an increase of one percent per year in both the agricultural labor force and output per agriculturalist. Given the conditions listed here, however, together with an income elasticity of demand of 0.5 for agricultural produce, total demand for this produce would grow only 1.5 percent per year, which means that a price-depressing agricultural surplus would come into existence and persist until the growth rate of agricultural output settled to a level commensurate with the growth rate of demand for this output. A portion of the agricultural population would therefore have to transfer out of agriculture and into nonagricultural activities, or the agricultural population would suffer a decline in relative and absolute average income.

In all of this we have taken account neither of price elasticity of demand nor of net foreign demand for agricultural produce. As a rule, however, price elasticity of demand is low, so that a decline in the relative level of the prices of agricultural staples does not greatly increase their domestic consumption. An increase in foreign demand can offset the failure of domestic demand to grow adequately, but it is unlikely to do so. Under actual conditions foreign demand for any particular nation's agricultural output is likely to grow very slowly. Indeed, it is because world demand for the agricultural output of underdeveloped countries, even for specialties, grows so slowly that many of these countries must also develop manufacturing exports if they are to acquire the foreign exchange they require to pay for needed industrializing imports.

There is a limit to this process of adjustment: The fraction of the labor force engaged in agriculture is unlikely to decline much below 5 percent, even in the absence of net exportation of agricultural produce. Indeed, should population continue to grow and agriculture become subject to diminishing returns, the fraction of the labor force required in agriculture would rise unless a solution could be found in agricultural imports. As we shall show later, even in today's underdeveloped world completion of the process may take many decades, as it did in the developed world.

The absolute size of Europe's agricultural population diminished slowly. Migration to nonagricultural communities did not suffice at first to carry the equivalent of all natural increase out of agriculture and the countryside. In only a few countries (England, France) did net outmigration early become great enough to do this. A number of countries did not reach this level of outmigration until in the late nineteenth or early twentieth century, and it was not until early in this century that the agricultural population of the United States declined.

Outmigration is not likely to reduce the agricultural population of underdeveloped countries until the next century, because natural increase and the agricultural fraction of the labor force remain too high. Let's suppose that at the start 80 percent of a nation's population is dependent on agriculture and 20 percent on other activities. Suppose also that a nation's total population is increasing 2 percent per year, and its nonagricultural population 4 percent per year. More than 70 years must pass before the absolute size of the agricultural population is below the initial level, at which time its relative size would be about one-fifth of the total. Should the nonagricultural population grow 5 percent per year, only 40 years would be required. Should the total population grow only one percent annually, a 4 percent annual growth rate of the nonagricultural population would begin to reduce the absolute size of the agricultural population in about 20 years.

Demographic relations and economic factors both condition how long it takes to reduce a country's agricultural population in size. The main economic relations are P', the rate of natural increase of the total population P, U', the rate of increase of the nonagricultural population U, and the ratio U/P. When U/P is low, U' tends to be higher, *ceteris paribus*, than when U/P is high; when U/P is low, U can draw relatively heavily upon P, which is relatively large, whereas when U/P is high, U can no longer draw heavily upon a shrunken P but must count relatively heavily upon the natural increase of population U. In general, as U/P increases, U' tends to fall until it approaches P' and even approximates zero if P' descends to zero. In some of today's underdeveloped countries, U/P is lower and P' higher than in the countries of Western Europe in the early nineteenth century.

Economic factors lead us to ask if U' can long continue at a level of 4 percent with P' at 2 percent, half as high as U' is assumed to be. For if the rate U' is too high, it will be accompanied by a decline in the growth rate of output and an increase in urban centers in both complete and partial or disguised unemployment. Thus, as Colin Clark infers from past experience, a country's nonagricultural labor force can grow 3 or 4 percent per year with good results, but not as much as 5 percent. In recent years Japan has been able to maintain with good results a rate of 4 or more percent. Between 1926 and 1939 Russia achieved a rate of 6 percent, but with adverse effects upon productivity. In the United States between 1860 and 1910, the nonagricultural labor force increased about 3.8 percent per year, and the urban population about 3.2 percent per year. At the same time the total population was increasing about 2.9 percent per year, and the urban fraction of the population rose from 20 to 46 percent. Corollary to past experience relating to the rate of growth of urban and nonagricultural populations is that relating to outmigration of the agricultural population. In European countries in the past this outmigration rate has usually not continued for long at a level above one percent per year, but the American experience is exceptional. The agricultural labor force declined about 2 percent per year from 1920 to 1960, and the farm population about 1.75 percent. But the rural population did not decline in that period; instead it increased about 28 percent, though the fraction it constituted of the total population declined from 48.8 percent to 37 percent. The nonfarm component of the rural population rose from 38 percent in 1920 to 76 percent in 1960; many chose to live in the countryside and commute to employment elsewhere.

Several conditions limit the rates at which a country's nonagricultural and urban populations can continue to increase, especially *after* the absolute size of the agricultural population has begun to decline. (1) The overall rate of population growth, P', sets a demographic limit, for the lower it is the sooner U', a given growth rate of the nonagricultural population, exhausts the capacity of the agricultural population to supply recruits to the nonagricultural sector. (2) There is also an associated economic limit. A shrinking agricultural population may not be able to increase output per agriculturalist rapidly enough to meet the growing need for produce. To illustrate: Earlier we assigned values of 2 and 4 percent per year to P' and U'; we set U/P initially at 0.2, and we assumed that if average income y grew one percent per year, per capita demand for agricultural produce would grow 0.5 percent per year and total demand for produce 2.5 percent per year. Given these conditions, at the end of 50 years total population would number 269, of which 127 would remain in agriculture; at the end of 60 years the figures would be 328 and 118, and at the end of 70 years 400 and 89. During the sixth decade the agricultural population would decline only from 127 to 118, or 7 percent, but in the seventh decade from 118 to 89, or 25 percent, and in eighth decade 70 percent. During the sixth decade output per agriculturalist would have to rise by 2.9 percent per year, and in the seventh decade to it would have to rise to 5.0 percent.

(3) Increasing output per agriculturalist almost certainly presupposes increasing investment in agriculture and thus adds to the growing capital requirement imposed by an increase of 4 percent per year in the urban population. The inputs essential to meet all these urban and nonurban requirements would probably exceed in value 12 percent of the national income. The degree of availability of all forms of capital thus sets a limit to both the rate of outmigration from the agricultural sector and the rate of growth of the nonagricultural labor force and urban population. If the annual rate of population growth were lower, say one instead of 2 percent, less capital would be absorbed by population growth as such and more would be available per capita to make possible increase in output per agriculturalist and equipment of the growing urban population. Should capital be lacking, rural outmigration would be checked and urban inmigration would tend to be accompanied by increasing urban unemployment. There is much evidence of this in underdeveloped countries, where urban populations are growing 4.5 percent per year, mainly because the urban as well as the national rates of natural increase are high.

(4) Motivation to move out of the agricultural sector into the urban sector assumes two forms. First, if the amount a farmer must pay labor is too high in relation to the productivity of this labor, he will tend to reduce the amount of employment he offers, which means that the resulting unemployed must find support elsewhere. Before 1940, according to Colin Clark, the critical ratio of wages to average output per person employed in agriculture was around 0.5; when the actual ratio exceeded 0.5 agricultural employment tended to be reduced. Second, whether a representative member of the agricultural labor force is inclined to move out of this labor force and into the nonagricultural labor force is conditioned by the ratio of agricultural wages to nonagricultural output per head. When this ratio falls below a critical level—Clark put it at around 0.4—nonagricultural employment becomes attractive enough to draw migrants. Various circumstances may condition the critical levels of these ratios and man's response thereto, but deviation from the critical levels influences the propensity to move out of the agricultural and associated rural sectors.

The high rates of population growth characteristic of many underdeveloped countries affect both their patterns of internal migration and the degree to which they can reduce the economic distance separating them from the developed world. First, the urban population of the under-developed countries has been growing about 4.5 percent per year, or more than twice as fast as it did in representative European countries in the second half of the nineteenth century. The resulting increase in the *proportion* of urban population in today's underdeveloped world is not much higher, however, than was the corresponding increase in nine-teenth-century industrial countries. Underlying the differences between trends in today's underdeveloped world and those in industrial lands dur-ing the nineteenth century is a great difference in the rate of natural increase; this is two to three or more times as high in today's underdevel-oped countries as it was in most European countries in the nineteenth century. Urban population is growing so rapidly in the underdeveloped world because urban natural increase is so high. The capacity of cities in the underdeveloped world to absorb immigrants from the countryside is correspondingly limited, with the result that outmigration affords little or no relief from rural population pressure, which is being rapidly inten-sified by the high rate of rural natural increase.

Second, because average incomes in the developed world are eleven or more times higher than those in the underdeveloped world, there is little likelihood that average incomes in the latter will ever closely ap-proach those in the developed world. To illustrate: Suppose that average incomes increase 3 percent per year in the underdeveloped world but only one percent in the developed world. Then, given that average in-comes are twelve times higher in developed than in underdeveloped countries, 60 years from now the corresponding ratio will still be 3.7 to 1. There is little likelihood, however, that average incomes will grow any faster in the underdeveloped world than in the developed, because the rate of population growth absorbs the very capital needed both to increase average income per head and to modernize the urban-rural structure.

2.3. DETERMINANTS OF POPULATION DISTRIBUTION PATTERNS

In the preceding section we looked at population growth and migra-tion, and the factors that conditioned the degree to which populations engaged in nonagricultural, predominantly urban activities. In this sec-tion we shall consider some of the factors that condition the patterning of population distribution. Population-distribution patterns, whether over a country or within a population concentration (town, city, metropolis, megalopolis), are not entirely determined, but they are subject to con-straints. Men choose from among a range of alternatives, given the prevailing preferences and the trade-offs among alternative combinations. This range has increased over time, though partly at the cost of alternatives that were available when numbers were smaller and otherwise distributed and the mode of life simpler and less swamped by affluence.

2.3.1. Natural Resources

In the past most populations were anchored by the needs to be near food and mineral sources, waterways and other modes of transportation (means complementary thereto), and conditions favorable to communication. Today, with one agriculturalist able to feed as many as 30 to 40 persons, only a very small fraction of the population is bound to arable land. Increase in output per person in other extractive industries has helped to reduce its population-concentrating power. Improvements in transport (see Section 2.3.2 below) also have increased man's range of choice.

Man has become less anchored in space because he has been able to economize on nonubiquities (that is, nonubiquitous resources) and their complements and to substitute ubiquities (that is, relatively widely dispersed resources) for nonubiquities, but now he is more dependent on certain nonubiquitous and sometimes nontransportable resources. Water that is both potable and otherwise usable has become increasingly significant as demand has increased for this resource, so limited in accessibility and amount. Regions that remain free of air pollutants by virtue of terrain and air movements will increase in value. Perhaps of greatest importance will be regions endowed with natural amenities, the value of which tends steadily to rise as economic activities become mobile and the amount of discretionary time and income increases.

2.3.2. Transport and Economies of Concentration

These two forces jointly condition population distribution (1) *over* space and (2) *within* the boundaries of areas where population is concentrated.

1. Increase in economies of scale at the plant level, together with the emergence of (1) interplant and interactivity complementarities and (2) the need to internalize favorable external effects (that is, externalities) within sets of plants under common ownership, increased the number of workers attached to given plants and of plant complexes benefiting from propinquity to one another. Concentrations of population resulted, both from the assemblage of more and more workers and their families and from the corresponding increase in the number of persons (together with their families) who supplied private and public services to the industrial population and to persons in the immediate hinterland. The

size of cities and other population concentrations grew accordingly, especially in the present and the preceding century. Though economies in the supply of public services probably did not greatly accentuate these centripetal tendencies, still, by preventing increase in service costs such economies averted what might otherwise have been a drag on the forces making for population concentration.

Economies of scale at the business administrative level were less conducive to concentration in the aggregate than those at the plant level. For the impact of business and administrative economies is felt mainly at points where administrative units are centered, usually in conjunction with units that benefit from propinquity and that specialize in the service of administrative units. Moreover, persons engaged in overall administrative activity are better paid, as a rule, than those engaged in more basic productive activities. Hence activities tend to be carried on in locations where labor-oriented costs and corresponding styles of living tend to be lower.

Given that trends toward population concentration are dominated by economies at the basic-production level rather than by those at the administrative level, one may infer that future trends will be conditioned by events at the production level, and by the relevant complementarities that emerge and persist. For a number of reasons, however, continuation of past trends is unlikely. First, economies of scale may be subject to modification, and scale itself to miniaturization. In the past they developed almost autonomously, because there was little or no direct effort to control them; but today there are directed tendencies toward miniaturization in such fields as electronics, weaponry, and oil refining; and they probably can be developed in many other lines. Second, as growth of per capita output in goods production keeps pace with the aggregate demand for goods, the relative number of workers in goods production will diminish, and so presumably will the absolute number present at any one point, now that plants are easily relocated. Third, given the relatively high income elasticity of demand for services and the absence of notable economies of scale in their production, the trends in the production of services will not be toward population concentration after average income passes a critical level. Fourth, as the cost of adverse externalities associated with population concentration is made incident upon the production units generating these externalities, some of the impetus toward concentration operative in the past will disappear. In the future, therefore, the pressure from economies of scale for population concentration will probably be much lower than it has been in the past, particularly in developed countries.

2. Transport has played a dominant role in the evolution of city size

and location and, as we shall investigate later, in the distribution of activities within cities. Improvement in land-borne and air-borne forms of transport and their addition to water transport have freed cities from the need to be situated along waterways (as late as 1900 every American city larger than 250,000 was situated along a waterway). Improvements in intraurban transport have enabled workers to live farther from their places of work and thus dispersed population within the ever-extending perimeters of cities. Generally speaking, improvements in transport have facilitated population implosion and a form of population explosion—the assembly of people into larger concentrations of population and the spreading out of people within the ever more wide-ranging boundaries of these concentrations. Even so, the implosion will eventually limit the explosion, which depends upon the availability of suitable terrain.

Improvements in extraurban transport have enlarged the area from which a city may draw goods and services from outside its boundaries and also the area into which it may dispose of that which it sells to earn the means wherewith to pay for these imports or their equivalents (such as travel or vacations outside). The area a given city thus depends on corresponds roughly to πr^2 where r designates the radius running in any direction from a city's center and grows as the square of r. An improvement in transport, expressible in terms of a reduction in the cost of moving particular products a given distance, is equivalent to an increase in r, and thus makes possible enlargement in what later we shall call the *economic base* of a population concentration. It also makes possible fuller exploitation of any potential economies—of scale, complementarity, conglomeration—that depend for their emergence upon enlargement of the market; it may be said to do this by reducing what amounts to a "transport" tax.

Increase in the quality and decrease in the cost of transport may affect population distribution around cities in ways somewhat parallel to effects produced within cities. First, it permits individuals to combine various degrees of rural life with city-oriented economic activities. Of this we have evidence in the increasing ratio of rural nonfarm to rural population in the vicinity of cities and in the hinterlands adjacent to cities. Second, as the number of hours worked per year declines, especially in large cities, improvements in transport permit sustained stays in areas where nonurban amenities abound and thereby reconcile many to economic activities within larger cities.

Improvement in intraurban transport, together with decrease in its cost relative to incomes, modifies the density pattern and may reduce overall urban density. Colin Clark has a formula, $y = Pe^{-bx}$, where P denotes density at a city's center, y is density x miles from this center, b

is the rate of decline in density, and e is constant. With a decline in the ratio of transport cost to the incomes of those purchasing transport, b declines, the limits of the city are extended, and A, the area accessible to its population, increases. The ratio of A to a city's population is much less likely to increase when a city is already large, old, and somewhat confined by natural or man-made barriers than when an opposite set of conditions obtains. The ratio A/U (where U designates urban population) thus is conditioned by the strength of these barriers.

2.3.3. Means of Communication

Population concentration is conditioned by the degree to which interpersonal propinquity has been essential to communication; when people attach great importance to propinquity the number of people situated in large cities will be relatively great. The conduct of both private and public affairs is highly dependent upon the assembly, transmission, and analysis of information. Over time the means of communication have been much improved, with the result that the assembly and transmission of information have both become less dependent upon the propinquity of those involved. Computerization has greatly facilitated the analysis of information; moreover, now that the means of communication is often connected with the means of computerization, it has further reduced the need for propinquity. Extant and future changes along these lines will greatly reduce the importance of propinquity to communication and thus facilitate the devolution of authority and the decentralization of decision-making, because men can use modern communication and computerization to coordinate decision much as they now use the price system to bring initially inconsistent decisions into line with one another.

There is at least one obstacle in the way of the population-deconcentrating trends just described; the seizure of information by the growing modern police state or by clandestine organizations engaged in the acquisition of critical information for sale to competitors or enemies. Should these tendencies (so inimical to the hitherto virtually costless economic contribution of man's trust in his fellows) persist, the relative importance of interpersonal propinquity will again grow, and with it the influence of forces favorable to population concentration.

2.3.4. Intraurban Channels

Section 2.3.3 relates mainly to interurban distribution of population; the channels that condition intraurban activity are analogous to the means of transport and communication that bind cities into networks. An urban center is essentially a network of channels devised to transport men, matter, and information within its perimeters and to tie in as needed with other more or less parallel networks of channels describable as cities. Over these intraurban channels move individuals, information, products, water, air, waste, contaminants, and other effluents.

Intraurban networks set limits to city size much as interurban networks set limits to interurban division of labor and cooperation and thus conduce to the devolution of decision-making and the regionalization of economic and related activities. The capacity of any one channel to carry that which it is designed to carry is limited, and so is the number of channels that can be introduced into a finite area. At the same time R_c, the rate of flow of that in need of conveyance (and hence the equivalent of demand for capacity), increases at least as fast as P' plus g' where P' denotes rate of growth of population in an urban center and g'_c denotes the rate of growth per capita of c, that which is in need of conveyance. In other words R_c tends to grow faster than channel capacity K_c, with the result that c accumulates within the urban center. While it may be possible to dissipate some c, attempts at dissipation often are limited to changing the form of c, preferably to one more easily conveyable over channels. In general, the growth of R_c sets limits in two ways to the growth of an urban center, by overcrowding both channel capacity K_c and sink capacity S_c, the c-sinks in the hinterland for the c discharged outside the urban center. Initially, of course, these overcrowdings produce only limited deterioration in the quality of urban living, but this deterioration grows as R_c grows.

2.3.5. Structure of Authority

The governance of an urban center may be represented as dependent on modes of communication, the demands on some of which grow more rapidly than population. There may then exist a critical population magnitude, which if exceeded may reduce the effectiveness of a city's governance, with the result that an administrative limit is set to the tolerable size of a city. Given the existence of such a limit, its emergence will depend upon socio-psychological and related factors, modification of which could increase or decrease the critical urban magnitude. Growth of a city beyond this magnitude would result in increasing socio-economic costs—by decline in security, increase in disorder, falling off in average productivity, growth of parasitic classes, net emigration, and the like—uncompensated by commensurates gains.

Locating such critical magnitude other than by empirical observation of the behavior of a city's residents is not easy. In general, increase in a city's population should reduce the relative size of a resolute bloc that wants and is able to control the indifferent and random-voting majority. It can also increase the relative number of objective links between individuals that generate the illusion that the forces of governance are strong. On the other hand, city populations are made up of diverse interest groups whose essential loyalty to the central authority is susceptible of being undermined. Should this happen, it would probably be in terms of a breakdown in socio-political communication. Little work has been done on this problem in its modern guise, and much of what there is is ideology ridden.

2.3.6. Fixities

Short-run options respecting the distribution of population among and within cities are very limited, for the number and sizes of urban centers, the location of employment opportunities, and the capital and physical structures of existing cities are already essentially given. These fixities can be changed over time, but only slowly and usually in such manner that though the nature of the options changes the range of choices is not much enlarged.

1. Constraints on area expansion can be eased but not eliminated. Let C represent the number of urban centers in a country, C' the rate of increase in C, and U', as before, the rate of increase in urban population U. So long as U' exceeds C' average city size will increase, and with it overall urban density unless A, the area passing under city control, increases faster than U. In summary, while the density of crowded sections of older cities has been reduced through dispersal within widened perimeters, the trend in overall density has been dominated by forces that increase aggregate urban area through both the creation of new cities and extension of the perimeters of already established cities. Given a low rate of overall population growth and a correspondingly low rate of urban growth, overall density would almost certainly be reduced.

Pressure to reduce density comes primarily from increase in man's average income y. For man is essentially a *space eater*, at least during his productive adulthood. Whence D'_s, the rate of increase in demand for urban space, will approximate P' plus ay', where a is individual income elasticity of demand for space. The value of a will be high because landed space is a superior good, because man's mobility tends to increase as y increases, and because man's sense of being crowded tends to rise when D'_s exceeds A', the rate of increase in available and appropriable urban area. The overall value of a will not approximate 1.0, of course, since not everyone is so situated as to be able to respond to an increase in y by seeking more space. Indeed, alleviation of the sense of crowdedness is not generally possible in larger urban centers. In the United States, for example, in 1960 ground space per person for *all* uses in cities of a million or more inhabitants approximated only .046 acre, while that in places of 250,000 or fewer ranged roughly between 0.15 and 0.33 acres.

2. Urban structure and form cannot be modified rapidly. Decisions concerning urban construction and development are frozen in concrete, in corridors of structures, in thoroughfare patterns, and so on. They reflect past city form, shape future form, condition the spacing of buildings, location of activities, disposition of lines of circulation, and so on, and determine how growth creates form and thereby limits future growth. Complete escape from all this is impossible, but constraints can be greatly reduced through anticipatorial planning that emphasizes retention of flexibility, especially in newly created cities and towns.

2.3.7. Urban Network

Throughout most of urban history, the predominant orientation of most cities has been to their rural hinterlands, whose productivity and populousness mainly determined a city's size. The sole exceptions to this orientation were cities supported by tax revenue and ecclesiastical tribute and some towns engaged in large-scale, long-range trade and export industry (for example in Holland, where by 1500 over half the population was urban) and hence capable of drawing subsistence and raw materials from afar as well as from an immediate hinterland. Today, however, the old rural-urban relationship, and the limitations it generated, no longer hold; nearly every city is a node in a network, as in a more primitive way were the long-range trading cities in post-medieval Europe. No city is an autonomous unit that combines with its hinterland to form a virtually self-sufficient system. Instead it is a specialized unit, both supplier and customer to other cities, and with them a network of cities. This network, usually under the dominance of several of its members, imposes a system of order on its urban components. Networks thus subject *ex ante* planning of cities and encompassing regions to considerable though not complete constraint. The extent of this constraint will not be fully known until current theories respecting the genesis of these networks are better tested.

2.4. REGULATORY FORCES

In Section 2.3 we looked at conditions that we may say determine the pattern of population distribution—at the physical and economic parameters and variables that are subject as a rule only to low rates of change. In the discussion we implied that processes that behaved as if they were stochastic have played a considerable role in the evolution of patterns of population distribution, in that each location-affecting decision has modified the options still available. Essentially this has been true throughout the history of human settlement; for, while many towns were located where subsistence was abundant or particular needs (defense, shelter, river passage, port functions, trade) could be served, because some could be situated at any of a number of points in an area, chance might influence the initial choice and thus set in motion a sequence of choice-conditioning decisions.

In this section our concern is with the degree to which the state, or nongovernmental assemblages of socio-economic power, can intervene with a view to influencing the distribution of population among and within urban centers. In the preceding section we indicated that technological progress has freed man of many of the locational constraints operative in the past and thus has widened his range of choice regarding population distribution.

Establishment of a city or other population center and control of its growth entail establishment and control of an *economic base* for its intraurban activities. A city is not self-sufficient; it needs to import certain goods and services, to finance undertakings by its inhabitants outside its boundaries, and to meet commitments for taxation and other expenditures elsewhere. In order to acquire the means to pay for these imports, undertakings, and commitments, the inhabitants of a city must sell enough goods and services outside its boundaries. The set of activities that yields these exportable goods and services may be said to constitute the city's *economic base;* these activities may engage (say) 20 to 50 percent of a city's labor force—the fraction is higher in smaller cities. They correspond to the functions a city performs for others. The members of its labor force not so engaged satisfy the local needs of the city's population, and the ratio of their number to the basal labor force may vary widely, as suggested.

In the past very few cities attained great size as a result of an expanding economic base and the multiplication of ancillary and complementary activities. The few that did emerge were based on tax revenue, tribute, and the support of ecclesiastical constitutions; their growth may therefore be said to have been state supported—as is the growth of seats of government today. The bases of other cities originated in a node of needs to satisfy which a node of functions could be clustered because the situation of the city-to-be was good and evolved slowly. No base could grow rapidly, nor beyond a low level, given a hinterland circumscribed by expensive transport and an agricultural population capable of producing only a small surplus for the support of a city population. Only a city situated on a waterway that supplied economical transport and inhabited by artisans capable of supplying accessible distant markets could enlarge the base and support its manpower. And even then expansion was always in danger of being checked by war, pestilence, or failure of the food supply. After all, until only several centuries ago life for many was nasty, brutish, and short, and only man's toughness and very limited expectations made it tolerable.

Two primary conditions distinguish modern societies from earlier ones. (1) Private business concerns were for a long time too small and too short of capital to establish growing cities through individual or joint action. (The main exception to this was the trading enclaves that groups of traders, mainly Europeans, set up in the Middle East or elsewhere; but these enclaves did not really metamorphose into cities.) Most cities were products of many small actions by decision-makers of limited power. Growth and the distribution of population among them was presided over by chance, often so well disguised that it was later interpreted as plan or intent. Today there are many private corporations and combinations capable of founding cities, planning their structure, and otherwise functioning as powerful states.

(2) Until recently only the state could marshal the means and power to launch full-bodied cities. Many such cities were established, especially in Asia and the Middle East. Collective intervention is manifest also in the planning of cities over the past three or more millennia, planning described in the writings of ancient authors and their less ancient successors and evident in gridirons and other layouts in both cities now defunct and the original kernels of modern cities. Today states are economically far more powerful than in the past, but because most lack the political power to focus on particular situations other than in the guise of creating a government-supported industry (for example, sites for aerospace activities) their contributions are more diffused than formerly.

Control over employment within the private sector is much more concentrated today than it was several decades ago or in the more distant past. First, only a very small fraction of the population is engaged in agriculture, which is an industry characterized by virtually no concentration of employment. Second, with the concentration of plants and with a greater number of diverse activities under the control of a single corporate enterprise, the relative number of nonagricultural employees under one top management increases. As a result a very small number of enterprises may account directly for a large fraction of total employment and hence for the spatial distribution of this employment. In the United States, for example, 750 corporations accounted for about one-fifth of all employment in 1965. Even should employment in services increase relatively, the basic situation would not change greatly, though the sizes of both business enterprise and plant tend to be smaller in the services sector.

The economic base of a city is more likely to be dominated by goods production than by services production. Even so some cities, especially regional and state capitals and "financial" capitals, depend largely on the sale of services to customers outside the cities in question. Moreover, since service production is small in scale and this in turn makes it relatively easy for a city to be nearly self-sufficient in services production, the ratio of total employment to the number of persons employed in the production of goods for sales outside rises. A smaller economic base is then essential to the support of a city with a given labor force.

Given that economic-base employment approximates 30 percent of all employment and that the ratio is constant or slightly falling, a corporation could set in motion the creation of a city of about 85,000 people by creating an establishment that employs 10,000 people in economic-base activities. This number would support a total labor force of about 33,000, which would represent a population of 80–85,000, given a ratio of around 10 workers to 25 inhabitants.

Such a city would entail heavy capital outlays for housing and public purposes in addition to private capital outlays essential to providing employment for 33,000 workers. Governmental underwriting of capital flotation might therefore prove necessary unless a consortium of private institutions could advance the necessary capital, an amount that would be very small when contrasted with the annual flow of gross savings and amortization funds. Complete financing by a single corporation is likely to be forthcoming for so-called "New Towns," plans for which provide for only some of the commercial and industrial capital requirements.

2.5. CITY SIZE

Until relatively recent times, few cities grew very large (information on the size of cities in antiquity is uncertain). By way of a criterion of the probable, it may be noted that around 1800, according to Woytinsky, no city had so many as a million inhabitants, though inclusion of London's suburbs would have given that city over a million people. Rome and Constantinople are said to have had as many as a million people for short periods, though so high a number is very doubtful. Marco Polo reported Hangchow to have three million; in the eighteenth century Tokyo and Peking were reputed to be the largest. Presumably only taxation and tribute could support very large cities before the industrial and agricultural revolutions and the improvement of land transport. The size of a country's population long set a limit to the size of its largest city, as did quite finite hinterlands to the cities which they supported. Not only did population grow very slowly, as in Europe between around 1300 (when several centuries of revived growth came to an end) and the late eighteenth century; its growth was also interrupted a number of times by pestilence and famine and sometimes war—these interruptions are reflected in the occasional arrest and sometimes even diminution in the size of cities. Although by 1300 there were 100 thousand or more people in Paris and a number of Italian trading cities, the growth of the preceding century or more was slow to resume. Eventually, with recovery from recurring pestilence and other barriers to economic and demographic development, the populations of a number of European cities began to grow, some to considerable size. London's population rose to 200 thousand in the sixteenth century and to nearly 500 thousand by 1665. There was also urban growth in Asia.

The emergence of the great city as focal point of population concentration is hardly two centuries old. In 1800, according to Woytinsky, only about 1.3 percent of the world's population lived in cities larger than 100 thousand; in 1900 it was about 3.7 percent, in 1920 and 1960 about 9 and 19 percent, respectively, according to a United Nations estimate. In 1800 there were only 36 such cities. Of these, 20 were in Europe (including European Russia) and 14 in Asia. By 1900 the number had risen to 93; of these 44 were in Europe (including European Russia), 16 in Northern America, 21 in Asia, and 8 in Latin America.

Many very large population concentrations emerged between 1920 and 1960, but the proportion of the world's population in very large cities did not grow so markedly because growth of the urban population, about 175 percent, was partly counterbalanced by the high rate of population growth, about 61 percent. Even so the urban figure rose from 19 to 33 percent. Meanwhile the fraction in cities of 100 thousand and over increased from 9.2 to 18.8 percent, and that in agglomerations of 2.5 million or more from 1.9 to 5.7 percent. Moreover, the fraction of the *urban* population in large agglomerations increased, with the percentage in places over 500 thousand rising from about 30 percent to over 38 percent.

Urbanization and population concentration have been associated with industrialization and modernization. This association is borne out by the data in the first column of Table 2-1, even though some regions (Australia, parts of Latin America) are relatively more urbanized than one might infer from their industrial structure. The association is borne out also by the increases in population between 1920 and 1960 in places over 20,000 (columns 3 and 4). The association is suggested indirectly also by the relatively more rapid growth between 1920 and 1960 of population

Table 2-1

Rural-Urban Composition, Actual and Projected, 1920–2000

Region	% Urban		% in localities with 20,000 or more inhabitants		
	1960	2000	1920	1960	2000
World	33	51	14	25	38
More Developed Areas	59	80	30	46	62
Europe	58	71	35	44	55
Northern America	70	87	41	58	72
Soviet Union	49	85	10	36	63
Oceania	64	80	37	53	59
Less Developed Areas	23	43	7	17	32
East Asia	23	40	7	19	33
South Asia	18	35	6	14	26
Latin America	49	80	14	33	54
Africa	18	39	5	13	28
More Developed Regions	60	81	29	46	63
Less Developed Regions	20	41	7	15	31

Source: Growth of the World's Urban and Rural Population, 1920–2000 (New York: United Nations, 1969), pp. 31, 59, 73.

in inland cities of over 500 thousand inhabitants than in seaport cities of this size, for inland cities respond more to modernization than do seaports because they are affected by improved land-borne transport and increases in the relative importance of domestic trade. The percentage of big-city population in seaports declined one-third in less developed regions, whereas in developed regions it changed very little.

The absolute rate of increase in urban population is also associated both with the overall rate of population growth and with the degree to which the countryside has been emptied of actual and potential surplus population. Between 1940 and 1960 the urban population grew 2.6 times as fast as the total population in the developed world and 3.3 times as fast as in the underdeveloped world. Over the same period the ratio of population growth rate in places of 20,000 or more to the growth rate of the whole population was about 3.3 to 1 in the underdeveloped world, compared with 2.5 to 1 in the developed world. Meanwhile population in smaller places and rural areas grew very little in the developed world but about 1.0 percent per year in the underdeveloped world. A similar pattern of growth is anticipated for the period 1960–1980.

The urbanization trends of the past 40 years are expected to continue as industrialization progresses; if so they will extend the urban fraction of the population in developed areas to 80 percent or higher, and to above 60 percent that in cities of 20,000 and over. The percentages are expected to increase even more rapidly in developing areas, though not enough faster to elevate above a level about half that anticipated for the developed areas. The trends are indicated in summary form in Table 2-1 in the contrast between columns 1 and 2 and between columns 4 and 5. By 1980, according to United Nations projections, about 16 percent of the world's population will be in cities of 20 to 500 thousand and about 15.4 percent in cities of 500 thousand or more. Should the same trend toward agglomeration prevail, by 2000 these percentages will rise to roughly 19 and 20.

The prospect of urban growth should not divert attention from the growth of rural population in countries with high rates of population growth. Rural population in developed regions had begun to decline by 1940; by 2000 it is expected to be only about seven-tenths as large as in 1960. In less developed regions the rural population increased 48 percent between 1920 and 1960; if between 1960 and 2000 it increases 80 percent as anticipated, by 2000 it will number over 2.9 billion, more than twice what it was in 1920 and nearly as large as the world's total population in 1960. It is probable, therefore, that in many underdeveloped countries surplus agricultural population will long persist, particularly if the so-called "green revolution" results in great increase in output per agriculturalist as well as in yield per acre. By the year 2000 the rural population associated with the labor force required to feed the world's population should not exceed 25 percent of the total, or about 1.5 billion, if that many.

> We are pieces of earth—selectively sublimated
> pieces, it is true, of peculiar composition
> and still more peculiar mechanical properties—
> but nevertheless pieces of earth, moving
> about on the earth.
>
> A. J. LOTKA

Man's physical environment embraces the atmosphere, the hydrosphere, the lithosphere, and nonconventional sources of energy (solar, wind, geothermic, tidal). Under atmosphere one may include air, space, weather, climate; under lithosphere land, soil minerals; and under the hydrosphere water and marine resources. These three spheres are interrelated in that substances move from one to another. Substances also move in and out of the biosphere, which, though it includes all living matter, is but an infinitesimal fraction of the three spheres upon which it is dependent. Man's life is thus connected with other life forms in the biosphere and with the three spheres comprising his inorganic world. Man has some capacity for modifying the composition of the content of these spheres. For purposes of exposition we shall divide man's natural environment into organic and inorganic spheres and then examine his relationship to each. Man is directly dependent for life upon certain components of his inorganic environment—especially water and air—upon his organic environment

CHAPTER THREE —the animals, plants, and organisms that

Population and the Natural Environment

make the inorganic environment subservient to his needs—and upon the ecosystems into which components of this environment are organized.

Man's consciousness of his relationship to his natural environment changes, but his ultimate dependence upon it does not. Empirical aspects of this dependence also change, even as does man's conceptualization and experience of "Nature." It is true, as R. W. Gerard observes, that "man has, in fact, largely cut himself off from the external environment and created a hothouse internal environment in which he lives" overwhelmingly at the symbolic level, and "in a man-made sea of meanings." But it is also true, as René Dubos states, that man's strength will wane, as did that of Anteus, should he lose "contact with the biological ground from which he emerged and which still feeds him, physically and emotionally."

In this chapter I shall deal with man's dependence upon and exploitation of his organic environments. Increase in man's numbers affects his environment in general, especially the ecosystem of organisms that bear chlorophyl, serve as food chains by converting plant life into food for man, and decompose lifeless organic material. Today increase affects even the air and water that cleanse man's habitats. I shall postpone discussion of the effects and implications for socio-economic policy until Chapter 8.

Man's interest in his immediate environment may have diminished, but his interest in environment in general has increased because local, regional, national, and world environments have all entered into his orbit of concern. Many factors have contributed to this: the growth and spread of world population; increase in the volume and rapidity of movement of people and goods; advances in knowledge, technology, and methods of production; and multiplication of the spillover effects, many of them costly, of what are or appear to be localized activities. Not surprisingly it is now common to think of our planet as *Spaceship Earth*—an essentially closed system from man's point of view—and of man's area of activity as the *homosphere*—a component of the biosphere and with it dependent upon inorganic components of the spaceship that cannot draw upon other systems for needed matter in greater measure than it does now.

It was not always so. In the past man's image of his relevant world was quite confined. For example, in Greco-Roman times men thought of the *ecumene,* or inhabited world, as but a portion of the physical world (which some conceived of as a disc and others as a sphere). Moreover, despite trade among countries comprising the *ecumene*—for example between India and China, or between India and Mesopotamia and later Rome—peoples were not considered to be knit together by international commerce and migration. Obstacles in the way of the movement of goods, people, and information were too difficult to be surmounted at little cost. Moreover, numbers were too thinly distributed, there were large clusters only here and there. Man's physical environment was not, therefore, thought of as a world environment to which world population was adjusting; and economic and cultural significance was attached only to a fraction of the constituents of the physical environment deemed important today.

Man may be said to draw upon his environment for the matter and energy that sustain him, only to degrade both, some so completely as to render them forever useless to other men. Life may therefore be viewed as a contest for available matter and energy, a contest that tends to become more intense as increases in man's numbers and consuming power threaten to reduce their availability. This contest is more intense now than it was when the prophet Isaiah observed that "all flesh is grass." For today more than ever before life consists in converting environment into flesh and artifacts, now many times what they were in a pastoral society. Whence, as A. J. Lotka noted, "man's industrial activities are merely a highly specialized form of the general biological struggle for existence." The struggle tends to be cushioned somewhat, at least in the short run, whenever man discovers how to transform neutral or uncongenial elements in his environment into useful elements.

Several caveats are in order before we take up the content and role of man's organic and inorganic environments. First, the line between man's physical and natural environments is somewhat arbitrary in that the shape and content of man's organic and inorganic world reflect the past incidence of man's activities. Second, the degree to which man considers components of his environment scarce is largely a function of culture and civilization, of the forces that shape his wants and of the degree to which less abundant components of his environment can be replaced by less scarce components at the level either of production or of consumption. Third, additional supply of that which man wants comes into existence only as the growth of effective demand warrants increase in the output of that which is augmentable. Potential supply, say, of rice or wheat becomes actual only as the production and sale of additional increments of output are profitable. Accordingly, in what follows profitability—the excess of returns over costs—needs always to be included among the determinants of the flow of useful ingredients of man's natural environment.

3.1. THE ORGANIC ENVIRONMENT

Until recently man's direct use of his inorganic environment was limited; he could draw upon it for shelter and nonsubsistence, but not for subsistence. It has been estimated that around 1700 about seven-tenths or more of the expenditures of Frenchmen and Englishmen went for things derived from the plant and animal kingdoms. They depended upon organisms to convert inorganic matter either into something edible (such as grain in the form of bread) or into feed for animals, which transformed this feed into animal products edible by man. They were dependent upon the plant world for fuel, fibers, and some building materials. Today man not only can draw directly upon the inorganic world for many of his emerging wants; he can also convert quite primitive organic materials directly into palatable and gastronomically attractive foods and thus shorten the food chain that links him to the inorganic world.

Two effects tend to accompany a shortening of the food chain. First, the supply of calories and perhaps other nutrients obtainable per acre of land or water will be greatly increased, and with it the food-supplying capacity of countries or regions. Second, the relative importance of some links in the food chain will diminish, together with their survival power in competition with man. As A. J. Lotka has observed, "civilized man has achieved the distinction of practically clearing the board of all foes of a stature in any way comparable with his own," with the result that "man's combat with his own kind has been forced to the center of the stage" as population pressure has increased and struggle at the industrial level has replaced that at the individual level.

It has been estimated that of the approximately 4 billion species of animals and plants that have existed during approximately the past 3 billion years, only about 4.5 million (or about one in a thousand) are now living. This extinction of species has been variously contributed to: by disturbance or destruction of habitat of a species, by interspecies competition, and by evolution itself, which before man arrived tended to fix the life of a species at an average of about 2 million years for a bird species and about 600 thousand years for a mammal species. The rate of extinction rose with the advent of man, particularly among species that he hunted or found useless, or that were dependent upon the continuation of conditions susceptible of change at man's hands. Indeed, of the bird and mammal species that have become extinct since 1600 A.D. three out of four owed their extermination to man's doings. "If present tendencies continue," R. A. Piddington concludes, "the world will soon be inhabited by man and his parasites. All other forms of life . . . will have disappeared into extinction." (The term *parasites* here means those forms of life that man deems useful, since he will attempt, not necessarily successfully, to preserve them and increase their numbers in keeping with his wants.)

So long as the basis of human society was predominantly organic, population pressure was in the form of numbers upon land, which was the main source of food, clothing, and housing. Such pressure became manifest many times in man's history. The problem was always the same: how to overcome a shortage of arable land and organic materials. For example, when Hellenic society faced a Malthusian challenge in the eighth century B.C., its members responded in different ways, but always to assure an adequate supply of organic products. Some city-states reduced population pressure by sending out colonies to Sicily, southern Italy, Thrace, and elsewhere. Sparta responded by subjugating her neighbors. Athens reorganized her economy, specializing in exportable agricultural and manufactured products, many of which were exchanged for cereals and other products imported from abroad.

Food shortage, the major component of the problems confronting Hellenic society, has persisted, growing in volume with population over the centuries and varying in localized intensity with the favorableness of crop yields. It confronted many currently advanced countries until relatively recently and has plagued multiplying populations in other parts of the world. Historians of the common man—usually overlooked in gaudy chronicles of war and exploitation—do not exaggerate when they think of his history as the "history of hunger." In 1960 a large fraction of the world's population—close to two out of three, according to responsible estimates—lived in regions where food intake was of poor quality and low in the high-quality protein derivable from animal products and legumes. This shortage reduces the capacity of the very young to learn. Persistant calorific shortage reduces the working capacity of those in the labor force. Undernutrition and malnutrition thus reinforce other forces that make for low output and low standards of life throughout much of the world. Escape from poverty begins with escape from organic constraints. As we shall see, however, escape is at hand, and for good if population growth is adequately controlled.

Man did not really begin to reduce his overwhelming dependence upon the organic world, at least in relative terms, until the nineteenth century. Then he began to add an inorganic base to the existing organic base of his society and economy—not for the first time, of course, but for the first time at a rapidly expanding rate. Still men continued to write of population problems in terms of the organic world, particularly of subsistence. Even today it is often asserted that solution to the so-called "population problem" consists in making the food supply grow faster than man's numbers. This statement has application, of course, to a large fraction of the world's population, but not to the so-called modern countries or to those really on the way to modernization, given modern patterns of consumption. Even sages of old recognized that man does not live by bread alone.

Because of the heterogeneity of the world economy, it is only possible to apply very abstract propositions to the whole of this world. International economic heterogeneity has long existed, but never in so pronounced a degree as it does today. The past two centuries have been an age of diverging incomes, an age marked until very recently by an increase in the economic distance between economically advanced and economically backward nations. In 1860, according to L. J. Zimmerman, the richest quarter of the world's population got 57.8 percent of earned income while the poorest quarter got only 12.5 percent; during the next century the percentages changed to 72.1 and 3.2. Around 1800 average income in the most advanced European countries was perhaps five times that in most of the world; today this multiple may be 20 or more. Indeed, around 1950 average income in underdeveloped countries may only have been about one-fourth or one-fifth as high as those in advanced European countries around 1800.

Table 3.1

World Population and Arable Land

| Continent | Population in 1965 (in milions) (1) | Area in billions of acres | | | Acres per person | | Ratio of Population in 2000 to that in 1965 (7) | 6 ÷ 7 (8) |
		Total (2)	Poten- tially Arable (3)	Culti- vated (4)	Culti- vated (5)	Total Arable (6)		
Africa	3.10	7.46	1.81	0.39	1.3	5.84	2.48	2.35
Asia	1.855	6.76	1.55	1.28	.7	.84	1.86	.45
Australia New Zealand	14	2.03	.38	.04	2.9	27.14	1.71	15.88
Europe	445	1.18	.43	.38	.9	.99	1.18	.84
North America	225	5.21	1.15	.59	2.3	4.51	2.24	2.01
South America	194	4.33	1.68	.19	1.0	8.53	2.15	3.97
U.S.S.R.	234	5.52	.88	.56	2.4	3.76	1.51	2.49
TOTAL	3,310	32.49	7.88	3.43	1.0	2.36	1.85	1.28

Columns 1 to 6 are from World Food Problem, II, p. 434.

Income divergence has been accompanied by occupational divergence, a reflection of change in the relative (though not in the absolute) importance attached to organic and inorganic products. For illustrative purposes American data may be used. In 1800 about 74 percent of the labor force was engaged in agriculture and 0.8 percent in fishing and mining; in 1960 the percentages were 8.1 and just over 1.0. Midway, that is in 1880, these percentages were about 51 and 1.8. Extractive activities, especially those having to do with food production, have declined by at least nine-tenths since 1800. Around 1960 15 percent or less of the male labor force was engaged in agricultural activities in the world's most advanced countries; in the least advanced the figure is over 75 percent. Presumably, given modernization and limitation of population growth, the fraction of the world's population engaged in agriculture can be reduced to 10 to 15 percent of the labor force and still meet the nutritional needs of the populations in most countries. In some countries this fraction can be reduced to less than 5 percent.

3.2. SOURCES OF ORGANIC PRODUCTS

Man's organic requirements, mainly nutrients, are drawn from two sources, seas and waters (fish products) and land (edible and inedible agricultural products and forest products). The yields of these sources vary widely, depending on the methods of cultivation and extraction, the degree to which relevant ecosystems are kept optimal, and the institutional arrangements that condition their exploitation. Yields vary also with the level and growth of the demand for output to which suppliers are responding—that is, to the Gross National Product and the growth of population and national income. As demand for agricultural produce rises, cultivation is extended and intensified, and it becomes more feasible to develop and adopt improved methods. Ultimately, however, the growth of sustainable output reaches economic limits that necessarily fall short of overly expensive technical limits.

How much exploitation of the seas and other waters can add to the total output of nutrients is subject to dispute (some expectations for the oceans resemble the expectations of cargo cultists). Sustainable annual fish harvests from the sea have been put at 115 million to 2 billion metric tons, or enough to supply the minimum protein requirements of 2 to 33 billion people, but some question whether a yield of 200 million tons can be sustained. This yield (if attained), together with slightly more than 50 million tons from inland waters, would supply the protein requirements of only about 4.25 billion people, which is roughly the world's current population. At the moment the sea harvest probably exceeds 55 million tons, and the yield of inland fisheries is around 10 million tons.

Should fish yields be pushed above biologically sustainable levels, the underlying fish population, and thus the annual yield, would be reduced. It is essential, therefore, that exploitation of the sea be subject to rules similar to those having to do with private property, so as to optimize the harvesting of the sea. Such rules need to cover the supply of fish with feed when that is practical, as it is in inland ponds that fish function as converters of grain, meal, etc., into edible flesh.

Nearly all of man's food other than fish is derived from the land through agricultural activity. Since population capacity depends upon the food supply, it therefore depends upon the amount of cultivable land and the efficiency with which it is cultivated—that is, equipped with productive plants and suitably watered, fertilized, and tilled. Current food production is susceptible of great increase because not all arable land is cultivated, and because not all of this is well cultivated.

Table 3-1 shows the distribution of the world's potentially arable land, about seven-tenths of which is in the arid or semiarid tropics or in the semihumid tropics (where wet and dry seasons alternate). Of the 7.9 billion acres estimated to be potentially arable, the growing season is unlimited by temperature or lack of moisture in but 1.24 billion; in 3.22 billion acres the growing season is limited by lack of moisture, and in 1.36 by low temperatures and lack of moisture. In 2.03 billion the growing season is limited by low temperature alone and will remain so unless frost-tolerant or rapidly maturing plants are developed. At present, therefore, less than 6 billion acres of the land estimated to be potentially arable are profitably cultivable, and much of the potentially arable land in the tropics may not prove so susceptible of high-level modern cultivation as today's anti-Malthusians anticipate. Presumably, therefore, even though only about 3.5 billion acres, or about two-fifths of the potentially arable land, are under cultivation, cultivation of all the land now uncultivated would not double the food supply, because man has tended to develop the lands best suited to his agricultural technology and economic constraints and favorably situated in relation to the courses of settlement he has pursued over the centuries. Nearly seven-eighths of the uncultivated arable land is in Africa, the Western Hemisphere, Australia, and New Zealand, regions with only one-fourth of the world's population. In Europe and Asia, where about seven-tenths of the world's population resides, over 84 percent of the potentially arable land is cultivated.

Since there are limits to fish production and small probability that the world's cultivated acreage will be effectively doubled, man must depend heavily upon increasing yield per acre. The 9 billion nonarable acres with some grazing potential could add only about 25 million tons of live-weight production per year to the world food supply, or 13 to 14 pounds per capita. Also, from this gain we must subtract about 7 percent of crop acreage that would be devoted to inedibles. Even if total acreage under cultivation were doubled and output per acre quadrupled, the resulting 700 percent increase in food production could be matched in about a century should aggregate consumption increase about 2 percent per year.

The prospect of famine-prone India is illuminating. After a long history of little agricultural progress, India could become self-sufficient in food grain production by 1986, given a 136 percent increase in output above the 1964 level. The "green revolution" is counted upon to supply most of this increase, if an acreage increase of about 10 percent can be added to an increase in yield per acre of over 110 percent. Yet even should India realize this target, limitations upon the augmentability of cultivable acreage and upon yield per acre will make continued self-sufficiency impossible should the population continue to grow even 2 percent per year and average income to rise one percent per year. One-shot improvements, such as preventing an estimated 20 to 30 percent destruction of stored grain by rodents, contribute, but cannot keep pace with growing demand. It is doubtful, of course, that India will prove able to increase its food supply adequately, given its variable weather, the crowdedness of agricultural land, the costliness of cultivating "miracle" grain, shortages of fertilizer and water, the limited capacity of small operators to make improvements, and the lack of complements to agriculture. The green revolution could provide considerable temporary relief, but only if all necessary conditions are met.

Augmentation of acreage under cultivation is restricted in several ways. First, incentive to develop this acreage is limited. If it is economical to meet a good share of local needs in land-rich regions through yield-increasing practices, the extension of cultivation will depend largely upon the expansion of foreign sales. Yet in Asia, where the already great pressures of numbers upon land will have doubled by the early twenty-first century, most incomes are very low, and consumption rises rapidly as incomes increase. Moreover, foreign exchange is preferred for other purchases than food while in America and Africa domestic supplies will suffice. In general, the tendency for international trade in foodstuffs is to be low, for countries prefer to depend on domestic sources, even when these are scanty. Net trade in grain is not likely, therefore, to exceed 4 to 6 percent of world production, even given some subsidization of grain exports by developed countries. Second, a great deal of the uncultivated arable land lies in the tropics; some of it is lateritic, and some is leached. Such soils require a tropical technology, and no such technology has been developed in labor-short, temperate-zone agricultural regions. Third, bringing new land into use entails considerable developmental expense even before investment in productive equipment becomes necessary. Fourth, potentially arable land is not effectively utilizable unless the water supply is adequate and temperatures are not too low. Fifth, the extension and intensification of cultivation are both conditioned by the price structure and the degree of play allowed economic incentive; in general, a sufficient spread must obtain between prices of inputs (fertilizer) and the prices of output (rice, wheat). Sixth, population growth may divert land from agriculture. For example, a great deal of land, much of it arable, has been diverted from farming to urban uses, transportation, and so on. Such diversion is especially high when urban migration is added to the natural growth of urban population. In the United States in 1950 the acreage devoted to cities, transportation, and public recreation approximated 17 percent of that devoted to agriculture; adding one person to the urban population absorbs between 0.1 and 0.5 acre. Should the addition of one person to the urban population in Asia absorb one-twentieth of an arable acre, and should the equivalent of Asian population growth in 1970–2000 settle in cities, something like 70 million acres, or one-fourth of the still uncultivated potentially arable land, would be diverted from agriculture. Given all the handicaps described, it is very doubtful that the acreage under cultivation will ever be double that now under cultivation.

The future of potentially arable land turns on the time horizon under consideration. Unfortunately, discussions can be muddied through the careless use of two time horizons. For example, it may be reasonable to assume that the world's food supply can be made to keep pace with numbers for 50 to 100 years, but it does not therefore follow that a sufficiency of food can be made available over a much longer period of time. Indeed, it is possible that the amount of potentially arable land may shrink because of changes in weather; it has been estimated that a three-degree rise in temperatures would melt ice in Antarctica and Greenland and hence raise the sea level by about two hundred feet, enough to cover the world's coastal cities and low-lying areas.

Given the difficulties in increasing world acreage under cultivation, the principal means of escape from food shortage in food-short countries lies in augmenting yield per acre. In fact, should this not be done, undernutrition and malnutrition—indeed, some experts fear famine—will be the lot of an increasing fraction of the population of the underdeveloped world before this century is out—especially in countries where fluctuating rainfall causes considerable year-to-year variation in harvest. Can yield per acre be made to increase as rapidly as growth of population and income—say 2 to 4 percent per year—in underdeveloped countries increases requirements? The 1970s bid for the first time in man's history to provide an affirmative answer to this question in much of the food-short fraction of the world. Nonetheless, continued confirmation of this answer depends upon cessation of population growth.

In the early 1960s yields per hectare varied greatly from country to country. Japan's rice yield, 4310 lbs. per acre, 2.1 times the yield around 1885, was 2.5 to 4 times that in many underdeveloped countries. The wheat yield in the United Kingdom—54.8 bushels—was 2.5 to 5 times that in the less developed world, while the corn yield in Canada was 2.5 to 6 times as high. The grain yield in North America was about five-sixths above that in the underdeveloped world. A particular advantage of the new varieties of high-yield grains—the so-called green revolution—is their suitability to low-yield countries where they would greatly increase yield per year and compel changes in production and harvesting that will detraditionalize and modernize agriculture. A disadvantage may be the vulnerability of "miracle" grain to crop-destroying disease.

Several courses of action are available, but each is limited by technological and economic constraints. Moreover, the success of any one course of action is conditioned by the degree to which complementary courses of action are taken. For example, if irrigation doubles or triples crop yields, the supply of plant nutrients must be correspondingly increased and measures for the control of pests and plant disease and facilities for cultivating, harvesting, storing, and transporting larger yields adjusted to the new situation. In summary, increase in yield per acre, because it depends on increases in complementary inputs, must be viewed as a system of interrelated inputs, not as a result of isolated inputs. Certainty of yield will depend in part on making "miracle" grain invulnerable to destructive diseases.

There are at least six steps that may be taken to increase output per acre.

1. Use of more fertilizer is of major importance. Production of grain, one of the major direct and indirect sources of man's calorie intake, tends to increase about ten kilograms in response to an application of one kilogram of chemical fertilizer plant nutrients.

2. Multiple cropping is possible, given suitable temperatures, sufficient water, and adequate inputs of capital, labor, management, and plant nutrients. It has been estimated that without irrigation multiple cropping could increase the gross cropped area by the equivalent of about three times the acreage currently cultivated; with irrigation it could increase it about five times.

3. Without insecticides and fungicides it is impossible to realize high outputs, even if other conditions are satisfactory, and without herbicides it is not possible to control weeds if labor is in short supply and expensive.

4. Mechanization saves both labor and land; in the latter capacity it makes the equivalent of more land available, both by eliminating the need to raise feed for draft animals and by increasing the number of days per year that land can be put to use when the growing season permits and water and fertilizers are available. Newer varieties that ripen faster may permit two to four crops per year, but such sequences cannot be successfully achieved unless seedbeds are carefully prepared, cultivation is timed effectively, and harvesting is carried out rapidly. These all require appropriate mechanization.

5. In the past improvements in plant and animal varieties have increased yields and extended cultivable areas, but it is only with development and application of modern genetics that plant and animal varieties could be bred to fit both environments and man's nutrient requirements. New varieties of rice, wheat, maize, and grain sorghum are especially striking. Some respond more effectively to water and fertilizer inputs and mature in less time than did old varieties; hence they are conducive to multiple cropping. Moreover, because they are not sensitive to length of day time, they can be planted any time during the year that water and temperature conditions permit. Hence not only may higher crop yields augment output per acre, they may also make also several crops per year possible.

6. An adequate supply of water that is satisfactorily distributed over time is essential to cultivation. When this condition is not met, irrigation is essential; when it is met only in part, irrigation often greatly augments annual yields. Because no more than about one-ninth of the world's cultivated land is now irrigated, the potential for irrigation appears to be considerable, given the volume of river runoff and an accessible volume of ground water estimated at 3000 times that contained in the world's rivers. Over one-half of the arable area of Asia, Africa, and South America requires or would benefit from irrigation. In places like North America and Australia large areas are arid because rainfall is inadequate in quantity or temporal distribution or both. Here also, therefore, there is scope for greater irrigation than at present, given effective demand for produce. There is not enough water within reach of irrigable areas to release the yield potential associated with full irrigation, even in the absence of the considerable waste of water that is the consequence of current irrigation and of man's seeming preference for grandiose irrigation projects rather than for small, practical, unspec-

tacular, economic projects. Some of the larger dams are sources of joy and profit to the earth-moving industry, but often disruptors of relatively stable watersheds. Illustrative of what could be on the horizon is the proposed $100 billion North American Water and Power Alliance involving 33 U. S. states, Canada, and Mexico, mainly for the benefit of the western United States and Mexico. Illustrative also is a proposal for taming the Amazon and neighboring rivers to create a system of lakes and thus make water much more widely available.

There are other yield-increasing practices. Fallowing, the opposite of multiple-cropping, is sometimes a moisture-conserving device and occasionally a fertility-restoring arrangement. Greater labor inputs may be indicated. Some methods of planting, such as paddy, may be superior to others, such as the broadcast method, under available conditions.

Effective development of these yield-increasing practices has been associated with complementary conditions that exist in developed countries but are generally absent from underdeveloped countries. Among these conditions Lester Brown mentions relatively high levels of per capita income and literacy, agriculture oriented to the market and kept profitable by favorable input- and output-prices, a nonagricultural section capable of meeting the needs of the agricultural section and of providing profitable domestic outlets for agricultural products, links between effort and reward that are close enough to stimulate activity and give appropriate direction to agricultural activities, and perhaps profitable foreign outlets for specialties or staples. Until these interrelated conditions have developed in sufficient measure, yields will be low and very slow to grow.

Despite the favorableness of conditions, until the 1930s grain yields increased slowly or not at all in Europe. In the 1930s they surged upward, and during 1951 to 1963 they increased 4.8 percent per year. Yields rose about 1.2 percent in Japan between the 1870s and the 1930s and 0.2 percent per year in the United Kingdom over roughly the same period, but in 1951–1963 yields in both countries rose about 2.6 percent per year. In India yields rose 2 percent per year in 1951–1963, though they showed no long-run increase over the preceding 50 years. For reasons indicated below it is not to be expected that upsurges of the sort experienced in advanced countries since World War II will continue. Innovations are exhausted and the substitutability of water, fertilizer, and other inputs for land finally tends to decline as labor or other inputs press upon the land.

The situation would be different in the low-yield underdeveloped world, should it escape the confines of a static, traditional agriculture within which little is possible. Here there is great scope for introducing methods similar to those that have succeeded in advanced countries and for exploiting high-yield new varieties of grain (rice, wheat, maize, grain sorghum). Yield increases of 100 percent or more are made possible by new varieties as shown by the increase in yield of selected Mexican wheat from 750 kilograms per hectare in 1945 to 1100 in 1955 and to 2600 (about 60 percent of the British yield) in 1969—an average increase of 5.3 percent per year. Realization on a country-wide basis of the yields made possible by the new varieties will depend on how fast and successfully the new varieties can be introduced and cultivated. It may also turn, in some countries, upon the growth of domestic and export demand, should supply begin to outstrip domestic demand. For in the near future much of Asia may attain self-sufficiency in cereal staples, and some developing countries on the margin of trading may become exporters. In the longer run, however, should population growth continue, domestic demand will overtake domestic supply.

There is an upper limit to the yield of a given crop that is technologically realizable in the absence of constraints imposed by pests, nonoptimality of temperatures or water supply, economic factors, and so on. Then, as James Bonner points out, "the limiting factor in the productivity of plants is the photosynthetic efficiency with which the plant converts light energy to energy stored in plant material." This upper limit, corresponding "to conservation in plant material of the order of 2 to 5 percent of the energy of the incident visible light," "is already being approached in those regions with the highest level of agricultural practice—in parts of Japan, of Western Europe, and of the United States." The average annual productivity of organic matter on fertile lands—about three tons per acre per year—suggests a kind of upper limit, given that about one-fourth of the matter could serve as food (an amount far below maximum wheat, rice, and corn yields attained on occasion in the United States). It may be theoretically possible to elevate limits such as the one described by Bonner by breeding higher efficiency into plants, but in practice it never pays to attempt to realize a technological maximum, since eventually cost of inputs exceeds the value of outputs. The economic feasibility of approaching any such maximum turns on the price of output, the prices of inputs, and the substitutability of variable inputs (such as fertilizer) for arable land.

The upper economic limits of crop yields do not determine population capacity. Since the calorific and other nutrient contents vary with the type of product, some crop combinations yield more calories per acre than others. The ratio of final calorific consumption to calorific yield also varies with type of crop, since some types of produce are more susceptible to loss through waste, spoilage, destruction by pests and rodents, and so on. The capacity of a crop to support population is conditioned, of course, by the number of calories finally consumed per crop unit. This number varies with a people's pattern of consumption; Americans, whose diets include large amounts of animal products, use about twice as much grain per person as a resident of the United Kingdom and about four times as much as a Pakistani. It is possible, however, that genetic improvements of the nutrient content of cereals and simulation of livestock products will modify consumption patterns, especially in countries such as the United States where overnutrition and sedentary habits are shortening life expectancy.

Since land suitable for food production is also susceptible of other uses, food production competes with other uses. For example, it is expected that by 2000 about 13 percent of the land in the United States will be devoted to recreation, transport, urban uses, wildlife refuge, and reservoirs (not all of this will be land well suited to crops). There is competition between cultivation and grazing and between use for crops and use for forestry. Use for crops tends to replace other uses whenever it gives rise to higher rents, as it may when the land in question is really suitable for profitable cultivation.

At present only a small fraction of forest land is about to be converted to crop land. In 1958 of the 10,635 billion acres in forest, 6678 billion were accessible, but only about half of these were in use. Much of this forest land is not very adaptable to agriculture, but it is expected that at least 1 billion of the 2 billion accessible tropical forest acreage will be diverted to the production of food and forage; this "loss" may, however, be offset by increased accessibility of the now nonaccessible 3 billion acres. Pressure upon forest reserves is being cushioned in two ways. On the one hand substitutes for lumber are increasing in importance: mineral products are replacing lumber in the construction industry and synthetic fibers are replacing cellulose. In the United States, for example, per capita consumption of timber products has not increased in recent decades, though today demands for lumber, veneer, plywood, and pulp are pushing up average consumption.

Water is the key resource. It is essential to all industrial and domestic activity, often the limiting agent in agriculture, and an important ingredient in the amenities, especially outdoor recreation. The amount of water required per ton of product in industry varies from something like one to two tons for brick to 600 tons for nitrate fertilizers and in agriculture from 1500 tons for wheat to 10,000 tons for cotton. In the aggregate, irrigation is the main absorber of water, followed by industry and municipal uses. For example, in the United States irrigation accounted for 83 percent of the water use in 1965, and municipal and industrial activities accounted for 12 percent; in 2020 these two percentages are expected to be 70 and 21.

Uneven distribution of the world's supply of water would give rise to water shortages even if the aggregate amount were sufficient. In much of the world rainfall is less than 20, even less than 10, inches per year, and this amount is unevenly distributed over the year. A major concern today therefore is the transfer of water from regions where it is abundant to regions where it is in short supply—witness plans to transfer water south from Alaska and Canada in North America, to divert some of Russia's streams, and to connect the Amazon and two other river systems in order to distribute water better for agricultural purposes (among other things). There is now an imbalance in many parts of the world between the distribution of water and the distribution of population. Water distribution will probably affect population in greater measure than at present, should it prove too costly or too disturbing ecologically to modify the current distribution and flow of water. In the very long run, however, some low coastal areas now plentifully supplied with water and hence attractive to population would be wiped out should the melting of polar ice raise the sea level notably.

The available water supply is mainly the result of rainfall, about 380 billion acre feet. Once rain reaches the earth it either returns to the atmosphere through transpiration and evaporation or collects in streams. Streams carry about 7 percent of the rainfall to the sea. It is on this *stream* flow that man must depend. We use only a very small fraction of it, even for irrigation, and we benefit in a limited fashion from evaporation and transportation, since so much of the rainfall takes place in areas of low habitation. Utilization of the water supply is much lower in the world as a whole than in the United States, where in 1965 about 6 percent of the daily runoff of 1200 billion gallons was used. This use rate is expected to rise to 10 percent or more during the next 50 years.

Man can increase the water supply available to him in three ways. First, since rainfall is but a small fraction of the moisture moving over the land, it may prove susceptible of increase through weather-modification practices. Second, some water may be obtained through desalination of sea water. Desalination assumes great importance now that cheap, abundant power of nuclear origin is in the offing and promises to reduce desalination costs. Third, since much available water escapes use, the effective supply can be increased by increasing the percentage put to use, especially the fraction of stream flow, and by reusing water that has not been unduly reduced in quality by earlier use. Good storage facilities reduce water loss that occurs as the result of rainfall seasonality.

The economic value attached to different uses of water varies considerably; it is estimated to be much higher in industrial, municipal, and some other uses, especially in advanced countries. Accordingly, in regions where water is in short supply, an increasing fraction of it may be diverted from irrigation without much effect upon agriculture so long as the amount diverted is small and can be partly made up by using more of the stream flow. Water shortages are likely to limit economic activities in the future as populations grow and the requirements of a rapidly expanding electric industry are added to those of agriculture, industry, and municipal uses. Pricing, rationing, and other arrangements might bring about better allocation of water among users and better balance between demand and supply, but they cannot greatly alleviate the pinch of a widespread water shortage.

3.3. MINERALS

Since modern economies rest upon a mineral base that is subject to depletion, minerals can become limiting factors. Whether they do turns on the ratio of projected rates of increase in mineral consumption to the reserves, since new deposits may by discovered and exploitation extended to leaner deposits. Moreover, while it may be possible to project consumption on the basis of certain assumptions, these assumptions change, particularly in developing countries undergoing industrial change. Indeed, mineral consumption is essentially a modern phenomenon, as is evident from the fact that there has been as much metal consumption since World War II as there was during all of human history before that time, and about half of that consumption took place between 1905 and 1938.

Modern industry is highly dependent upon minerals, but mineral-short countries can escape the constraints of their shortages through importation. These constraints are most pronounced in countries with small areas, though some regions of the world are much less well endowed than others. Japan is the most dependent of the modern industrial nations and is becoming more so. For example, in 1968 it imported about 100 percent of its oil, aluminum, nickel, and uranium; 85 percent of its iron ore; 72 percent of its coking coal; and large percentages of other raw materials. By 1975 some of these percentages will be higher. Even the United States, producer of large amounts of minerals, imports large fractions of most of the metals and metallic ores it uses. Countries that are heavily dependent on foreign sources will not only experience rising costs as a result of increases in world demand for minerals as industrialization grows and spreads; they may also encounter difficulty in importing materials from countries that decide to retain their minerals and base domestic industries upon them.

The prospect for fuel minerals is much better than that for nonfuel minerals. First, fossil fuels may last two centuries, perhaps longer, given the extent of coal resources. Second, a number of other sources may become available: solar energy, water power (which may prove the most important immediately), tidal power, and geothermal energy. Finally, there is nuclear energy, through atomic fission and fusion (as soon as fusion can be harnessed). These sources should supply several times ten kw. thermal (kwt.), which is the current annual per capita consumption in the United States, and the U.S. figure is six and two-thirds higher than the world per capita consumption.

The currently exploitable reserves of nonfuel minerals are not likely to last many decades, given expanding world consumption, but increasingly leaner ores may prove exploitable, given sufficient and cheap energy. Major innovations are required, however, to prevent upward trends in mineral costs associated with increasing need to exploit less rich ores. Indeed, some experts believe that it will be virtually impossible to increase metal production to levels that will enable a world population of 7 billion to live in a manner comparable to life in the United States today.

Weinberg and Hammond, among others, look upon cheap and abundant energy as the "open sesame" to a world of mineral abundance. They believe that at least enough energy can be made available yearly to supply 400 billion kwt., which is enough energy to supply 20 billion people with twice the average energy that Americans now consume each year. This amount of energy, with desalination and coveyance, will make seawater available for agriculture and other uses and as a source of hydrogen for the reduction of metals from ores. It will also enable each person to live at least as well as the average American now does, it is claimed.

There are limits, of course, to the amounts of nuclear energy that can be produced and used safely. Weinberg and Hammond point to the serious problems associated with radioactive waste, but they seem to believe that the fundamental limit is dissipating heat and the associated change in the earth's average temperatures—only .2°C., given an output of 400 billion kwt. Geological and metallurgical experts are less optimistic, even given fusion or breeder reaction; they point to the great costs of capital and the transmission of energy, to the enormous amount of unusable inorganic waste to be disposed of, and so on. The future of man's longer-run energy supply then depends upon his ability to develop and use nuclear energy in ways that are free of these problems.

Much of what has gone before may be encapsuled in a highly general formula: $P = py \div UE(1 - d)$. Here P denotes pressure of population upon man's inorganic environment, p and y designate total population and average income, U, the utilizable fraction of E, denotes the utility derivable from the total inorganic environment E; and d is that fraction of E that has been deprived of utility by man's past use of E (for example, through consumption of the stock of fossil fuel).

Pressure upon resources is the product of both the number of people and the average amount of use made of resources. For example, population density expressed in areal terms is incompletely represented by area divided by population, since interpersonal contact, use of space, and other concomitants of ordinary population density depend also upon a population's mobility. Mobility varies according to country and region, and has increased greatly over time. Hence if we define density as A/pm where A is area and m the average mobility of population p, we have a more complete impression of the use of space than we have if we merely write A/p. Similarly, if we write E/py we have a more complete impression of pressure upon E than if we merely write E/p. It is true, of course, that average income is an imperfect index of the average demand made upon environment, since this varies with a people's tastes, income distribution, current technology, and so on. Even so we may use y as an indicator of the average level of use of E, and y', or rate of increase in y, as an indicator of increase in average use.

Man's activities affect the substance of E, his inorganic environment, in two ways. On the one hand, through changes in his technology and tastes he has been able to draw an increasing fraction of the potentials of his environment into use. Increase in U, the fraction of E at man's disposal, reflects increase in the importance of man's environment. At the same time man uses up potential in his environment by changing its composition from a useful to a useless form, as when he exhausts supplies of fossil fuels. Man's activities may then be said to produce economic *entropy*, which is change from a more to a less useful state. The resulting loss is designated by d. In general, then, the environment effectively at man's disposal is not E but $U(1 - d)E$.

Pressure upon environment, P, increases with increase in p, y, and d, all of which have been increasing over time. Offsetting these increases has been such an increase in U that increases in d have been more than offset up to now. Increases in U correlate highly with increases in y, however, since common causes contribute greatly to increase of each. Accordingly, increases in y offset increases in U in considerable measure and reduce the effect of increases in U upon increases in P. In time, moreover, since E is both finite and made up in part of depletable substance, d may be expected to increase over time. Some increases in d—such as pollution of the environment or ecological disturbance—may, of course, prove temporary if they prove to be subject to reversal.

The impacts of U and d are often subject to ideological misinterpretation. Those who play down the significance of population growth for man's welfare tend to stress U and to argue that the rate of increase U' in U tends to offset p', the rate of increase in P. They overlook the costs that come in the wake of U' when it is accompanied by a positive and even relatively high P. Some of these costs, moreover, assume the form of d and increase it over time. It is possible, of course, both to underestimate the degree to which technology and changing tastes increase U and to exaggerate d and thus overestimate P and its rate of increase. It is also possible since P depends upon py, to attribute effects to increases in p that are really correlates of increase in y; this tendency is particularly pronounced in modern industrial societies.

In Chapter 6 we shall examine the implications of P and its determinants for man's welfare and for what are called population optima. At this point, however, we should note that d, together with thermal and other pollution, ecological disruption, and all other costs attendant on efforts to increase U', sets a limit to the physical and economic tolerance of increase in P.

And one man in his time plays many parts,
His acts being seven ages.

SHAKESPEARE

Drastic changes in the age composition of
the world's populations have been brought
about by fertility and the decline in
mortality. In advanced economies the relative
number of older persons has increased
greatly. In the United States, for example,
the percentage of persons 65 and over rose
from around 2 in 1830 to 8.2 in 1950. In
Western Europe these percentages rose from
a range of from just over 4 to just under 6
to a range of from close to 8 to nearly 11.
France was exceptional: because its birth
rate fell earlier the fraction rose from 6.47
percent in 1850 to about 11.8 percent in 1950.
In the underdeveloped world the number
of persons over 64 remains small, but the
relative number under 15 has risen in a
number of countries to 41 to 46 percent, a
figure comparable to that in the early
history of the United States when it was
easier to employ children productively. The
percentage for such children in developed
countries is roughly within a range of from
24 to 31 percent.

A society's age structure conditions such
characteristics as crude natality and
mortality, dependency ratios, potential output
per head, the distribution of political power,
youth-connected problems, and problems
connected with the "aging" of populations.

CHAPTER FOUR

Age Composition

These vary, as suggested, from the developed to the underdeveloped world.

4.1. THE GENESIS OF CHANGE IN AGE COMPOSITION

Changes in age composition are replicated in models, embodied in Tables 1-1 and 1-2, based on a United Nations study. They demonstrate that because age composition is a joint product of age-specific fertility and mortality rates, it changes as these rates change. For example, up to a point decrease in mortality and increase in gross reproduction affect age composition in the same way, by increasing the relative number of persons under 15 and decreasing the relative number in the 15–59 group. Table 1-1 depicts relationships in stable populations based on high fertility; these represent conditions in countries that are economically and demographically underdeveloped. The relationships depicted in Table 1-2 are characteristic of relatively and very developed countries.

What is the impact of change in life expectancy? Suppose that the Gross Reproduction Rate (G.R.R.) is constant at 2.5 and that various expectations of life at birth are combined with it. This amounts to combining a range of birth rates (37 to 43 per 1,000 persons) with various crude death rates. The actual level depends upon the level of crude mortality that emerges as stability of age composition approaches. The tables indicate that an increase in life expectancy reduces natality, augments natural increase, diminishes the relative number of persons 15 to 59 years old, and increases the relative number under 15, but has little effect upon the relative number 60 and over.

The effect of a rise in life expectancy upon natural increase depends upon the level the increase begins at. When the G.R.R. is 2.5, an elevation of life expectancy from 30 to 40 years raises natural increase by 8.7 per 1000, one from 40 to 50 years raises natural increase by 6.3 per 1000, and one from 60 to 70 by 4.1 per 1000. Increasing life expectancy beyond 70 adds little to natural increase since so much of a cohort's childbearing and births (about 93 percent in the United States) has already been supplied when expectancy is at 70 years. Indeed, if life expectancy rose from 70 to infinity, A. J. Coale estimates, natural increase per 1000 inhabitants would rise by less than 2. Thus, given a G.R.R. of 3 and life expectancies of 60, 70, and infinity, the rate of natural increase per 1000 persons would rise from about 38 to about 40. It is increase in life expectancy at young ages, such as has taken place in the underdeveloped countries in recent decades, that elevates natural increase. For example, given a G.R.R. of 2.5 to 3.0, an elevation in life expectancy at birth from 30 to 50 reduces crude natality slightly but raises natural increase by 15 per 1000.

An increase in life expectancy beyond 70 may increase the relative number of persons in the upper age groups, say above 50. Indeed, if death were avoided altogether and men were immortal, the fraction over 60 might be very high, though it need not be since it depends also on the *G.R.R.* The fraction over 60 in a society of immortals would be 41.4 percent given a *G.R.R.* of 1.5, but only 9.1 percent given a *G.R.R.* of 3. Undoubtedly, however, in a society of immortals, the *G.R.R.* would settle at a low level, not much above 1.0 at most. It is of course fanciful to suppose immortality; even now life expectancy at advanced years in developed countries shows little or no tendency to increase. Presumably new diseases and intensification of certain old diseases, especially those connected with pollution, are checking further decline. Moreover, today more than ever in the past less vigorous human strains are surviving into adulthood and middle age, only to succumb upon reaching the 60s and beyond.

When we turn to fertility we find that data in the tables reveal that as fertility declines, with life expectancy given, the relative number of persons under 15 in a stable population diminishes while those of persons aged 15 to 59 and over 59 rise. For example, given a life expectancy of 60.4 years, a decline in the *G.R.R.* from 2.5 to 1.5 increases those aged 15 to 59 and over 59 by 6.1 and 7.1 respectively while diminishing those under 15 by 13.2.

Changes in age composition associated with decline in fertility are partly offset by increase in life expectancy, usually a concomitant of decline in fertility. For example, given an expectation of life at birth of 40 years and a *G.R.R.* of 2.5, a stable population is composed as follows: under 15, 38.5 percent; 15 to 59 55.6 percent; 60 and over, 5.9 percent. Should life expectancy rise to 70.2 years and the *G.R.R.* descend to just over 1, the increase in persons 60 and over to about 21 percent of the population largely offsets the decrease in the percentage under 15 to close to 20, with the result that the fraction of those between 15 and 59 rises slightly over 3 points.

As I implied earlier, decline of the Gross Reproduction Rate is not immediately much reflected in the behavior of crude natality. Thus if age-specific fertility declines one percent in a population that is stable and has been growing 2 percent per year, the women of childbearing age will continue for 15 or more years to increase at a rate of 2 percent per year, and this increase will for a time increase the absolute number of births enough to offset the decline in fertility. Eventually, however, the age composition becomes completely adjusted to the decline in age-specific fertility. As a result the total number of births, crude natality, and mortality will eventually reflect the decline in age-specific fertility. A decline in natality and natural increase, though sufficient to reduce the Net Reproduction Rate (*N.R.R.*) to the replacement level, does not eventuate in a zero rate of growth until a number of decades have passed and the population has grown 25 percent or more.

4.2. AGE COMPOSITION AND NATURAL INCREASE

Turning now from the long-run impact of rise in life expectancy at different ages upon crude natural increase, we may note that a population's crude mortality and crude natality are both conditioned by its age composition. Age-specific mortality moves from an initial peak in the first year of life to a minimum in the 10–14 age group and then slowly rises to a maximum in the uppermost reaches of the age structure and life span. In the short run, crude mortality falls when net immigration or an upsurge of births increases the relative number of inhabitants in the lower age groups, which are marked by lower death rates. In time, however, the age structure takes on the shape compatible with prevailing age-specific fertility and mortality, and the crude death rate moves upward to a stationary level. The impact of an abnormal age structure upon mortality is transitory, and disappears with the advent of stability. In the longer run it is age-specific mortality that controls the crude death rate. In the real world, of course, adjustment proceeds slowly and may be subject to variation in fertility or mortality.

Fertility too varies greatly with age. It is generally at a peak among women aged 20 to 24 years; it usually is somewhat lower in the 25–29 age group, though sometimes it is higher. Thereafter the rate declines, but much more slowly in some countries than in others. Usually, though not always, it is higher among women 30 to 34 years old than among those 15 to 19; this reflects marital conventions in that in most countries a much larger fraction of those aged 30 to 34 than of those 15 to 19 are married. Fertility is very low in most countries among women in the 40s. As a rule, in countries with a *G.R.R.* below 2.0, 75 or more percent of all births are contributed by women 20 to 39 years old; This percentage usually is lower in countries with a *G.R.R.* over 2.0. Crude natality rises when for reasons of immigration or as a result of an upsurge of births 16 to 20 years earlier, the relative number of women in the 20s becomes abnormally large. This rise in natality is transitory, however, and in time the age composition of the female population becomes relatively stable, with the result that crude natality again depends entirely upon age-specific fertility rates.

4.3. AGE COMPOSITION, POTENTIAL PRODUCTIVITY, AND DEPENDENCY

Dependency ratios contrast the relative number of dependents in a population with the relative number of producers in the same population; they thus depend, with potential productivity, upon a population's age composition. A satisfactory dependency ratio will include all dependents, young and old, even though most ratios change in response to changes in fertility and mortality. Thus an unsatisfactory ratio, one contrasting only those under 15 with those 15 to 59, varies with fertility, as does a satisfactory one including all dependents. For example, with life expectancy at 60.4 years, a decline in the *G.R.R.* from 2.5 to 1.5 diminishes the ratio of those under 15 to those 15 to 59 from 41.4/52.6 to 28.2/58.7—that is, from 0.79 to 0.48. A corresponding decline in the *G.R.R.* produces a smaller decline in the ratio of all dependents—say all persons under 15 and over 59—to the total population. The percentage these dependents form of a population falls from 47.4 to 41.3 in a stable population when, with life expectancy at 60.4 years, the *G.R.R.* declines from 2.5 to 1.5; the number of dependents falls about 10 percent, whereas the number of persons 15 to 59 years old and supposedly of working age rises about 12 percent, from 52.6 to 58.7.

The ratio of the persons of working age to the total population is at a maximum when a population is both stable and stationary. This is true whether we define persons of working age as 15 to 59 or 15 to 64. This will not be true if we include in the working-age population only those aged 15 to 44, nor if we include among the age compositions those associated with declining populations, even though in a population that is declining slightly the relative number of persons 15 to 64 may be slightly greater than in one that is stationary. A declining population should, however, be ruled out of consideration under most circumstances since it cannot persist in such form as to ensure both permanency of the high ratio of persons aged 15 to 64 to the total population and adequacy of total population. (Greatly overpopulated countries are exceptions to this statement.) Whether the ratio of those aged 15 to 64 to the entire population is a satisfactory measure of average potential productivity depends, of course, both upon the degree to which productivity varies little with age over the age-range 45 to 64 and upon whether members of this age group have equal access to employment and hence are not denied employment by the state, trade unions, or corporate bureaucrats. This ratio would not be satisfactory if productivity were much higher among those under 60 than among those over 60, but this is no longer the case.

The dependency problem confronting high-fertility countries differs from that confronting low-fertility countries, particularly when mortality is relatively low in high-fertility countries. High-fertility countries are burdened with young dependents. With a *G.R.R.* of 3, dependents under 15 make up 43.1 percent of the population when life expectancy stands at 40, and 47.3 percent when life expectancy stands at 70.2. With a *G.R.R.* of 1.5 these percentages are 25.9 and 29.3. The resulting advantage of low fertility countries is only partly offset by their having relatively larger older populations. It is to be noted also that dependency is a much greater handicap to today's underdeveloped countries than it was to Western European countries in their early stage of development, because then relatively high mortality and relatively lower fertility than is found in many of today's underdeveloped countries held down natural increase and dependency ratios.

4.4. AGE COMPOSITION AND POLITICAL POWER

Men's interests, and the importance they attach to present and future, vary with age. Illustrative is inflation; its harmfulness tends to increase with a person's age. Older persons view many issues differently than younger persons: the financing of public expenditures; rules governing retirement; the composition of public expenditures; the weight attached to seniority in the distribution of employment, political rank, or preferment; the character of pension systems and social security; the ratio of fringe benefits in labor contracts to cash wages; and so on.

Changes in age composition may redistribute political power and hence modify the weight attached by governments to various concerns. An increase in fertility eventually increases the relative number of younger voters; a decline produces the opposite effect. The magnitude of these effects depends on the degree to which the young are given political power (as in the United States, where the voting age has been reduced from 21 to 18). Let us consider Table 4-1.

Given a population's age composition, the political outcome depends upon how men's interests, expectations, and sense of commonality of concern run. For example, suppose age 45 is the dividing line. Then the number of persons—and hence voters—45 or older tends to be exceeded by those under 45 when the rate of natural increase in a stable population exceeds about 5 per 1000. Given a stable male population with a life expectancy of about 71.2 years and growth rates of 0, 5, and 10 per 1000

Table 4.1

Age Structure of Representative Stable Populations

Proportions in Each Age Group, Given Value of P'

Age	Male					Female				
	−0.005	0	+0.005	+0.01	+0.015	−0.005	0	+0.005	+0.01	+0.015
0-14	17.53	20.53	23.75	27.14	30.65	16.64	19.64	22.88	26.29	29.84
15-19	6.11	6.81	7.49	8.13	8.73	5.81	6.53	7.23	7.90	8.52
20-24	6.24	6.78	7.27	7.70	8.06	5.95	6.51	7.04	7.50	7.89
25-44	26.16	26.71	26.94	26.85	26.44	25.08	25.80	26.19	26.25	26.00
45-64	26.45	24.46	22.35	20.18	18.02	26.07	24.28	22.31	20.26	18.17
65-69	5.71	4.96	4.25	3.59	3.00	6.04	5.28	4.56	3.88	3.26
70-74	4.80	4.06	3.40	2.80	2.28	5.36	4.57	3.85	3.19	2.61
74+	6.99	5.68	4.55	3.60	2.82	9.05	7.39	5.95	4.73	3.70
Total	100.00	99.99	100.00	99.99	100.00	100.00	100.00	100.01	100.00	100.00

Source: Ansley J. Coale and Paul Demeny, Regional Model Life Tables and Stable Populations (copyright © 1966 by Princeton University Press). Reprinted by permission of Princeton University Press.

inhabitants, the percentages that persons over 45 form of the entire population 20 or more years of age are 54, 50.2, and 46.7. Hence the ascendance of those over 44 is assured only if the true rate of natural increase is close to zero. If the vote is conferred on those 18 and over, then of the males 18 and over about 53 percent will be 45 and over in a stationary population based on a life expectancy of 71.2 years. Given a rate of increase of 0.5 percent per year, this percentage declines to 49.2. Accordingly, only if relatively more older than younger persons vote or the dividing line is pressed below 45 will the older half of the population retain political ascendancy.

4.5. YOUTH-CONNECTED PROBLEMS

There are at least three problems connected with the presence of a relatively high number of persons under 15, or 20, or 25 in a population that we should note here. First, when the relative number of young people is large, because of a high G.R.R., it becomes difficult if not impossible to make adequate provision for their training and education. Given a life expectancy of 60.4 years and a G.R.R. of 2.5, we have a population consisting of 414 persons per 1000 under 15, 526 aged 15 to 59, and 60 over 59. The ratio of persons 15 to 59 to persons under 15 then is 1.27:1; had the G.R.R. been only 1.5, this ratio would have been 587 to 283, or 2.08:1—over half again as high. Given a pupil-teacher ratio of 20 to 1, education alone absorbs the services of at least 4 percent of the labor force in the former case, but only 2.4 percent in the latter. Other costs associated with bringing up children would be correspondingly higher and would absorb capital and the services of adults accordingly. Evidence of the impact of these adverse effects of high fertility exists in most underdeveloped countries.

The ratio of children to adults also conditions the capacity of a society to assimilate and convert its youth into responsible members. This capacity is weakened by many circumstances, among them the fact that criminal and other forms of antisocial behavior are much higher among young than older persons. The capacity of a society to assimilate its youth depends, of course, upon nondemographic and demographic conditions, and the relative number of youth merely accentuates some of the problems. This capacity is higher in a rural than in an urban society, and in a slowly changing than in a rapidly changing society. The example in the preceding paragraph suggests that the task of assimilation might be half again as difficult with a G.R.R. of 2.5 as with one of 1.5.

Economic assimilation is much more difficult as a result of high fertility. When the Gross Reproduction Rate is high, it is harder for persons newly entering the labor force to find satisfactory employment. For example, a United Nations study suggests that in a stable population with representative labor-force participation rates, with a life expectancy of 50 and a *G.R.R.* of 3.5, withdrawals from the labor force because of death and retirement would number about 13.1 per 1000 active males, whereas new entries into the labor force would number about 45 per 1000. Whence the *additional* jobs required would approximate 32 per 1000. Under these circumstances it would be difficult to expand employment at the rate of 3.2 percent per year. However, given a life expectancy of 70 and a *G.R.R.* of 1.5, the rate of entry per 1000 active males (26.4) would exceed the rate of withdrawal (16.4) by only about 10. Hence, employment would need to be increased only about one percent annually instead of 3.2 percent. The probability is much higher, therefore, that those newly entering the labor force under the latter set of circumstances will find employment. Not only is a much higher rate of job creation called for when the *G.R.R.* is high; there is much greater need also for capital and other employment-fostering inputs, a need hard to meet when the rate of capital formation per head is as low as it is in high-fertility countries.

Even when the Gross Reproduction Rate is not so high, variations in it may later produce variation in the age structure and hence in the ease with which employment can be found by persons newly entering the labor force. This would not happen if the aggregate demand for labor always kept pace with its supply. In reality, however, the growth of the demand for labor and hence employment is affected by a variety of conditions as well as by the growth of the labor force. Still, it is much easier for persons newly entering the labor force to find jobs when employment is expanding faster than the supply of labor. This relationship can be affected by variation in natural increase, which eventually (say 18 to 24 years later) produces variation in the ratio of persons newly entering the labor force to the total labor force; because if the ratio should rise significantly because of an earlier upsurge of births, employment might prove harder to find, with the result that unemployment increased. An earlier "subnormal" number of births could produce an opposite effect. The ease with which employment may be found by those newly entering the labor force will affect their disposition to marry and form households several years later, and could thus affect the growth rate of the relative number newly entering the labor force when children born into these households had grown up and become job seekers. The complicated processes underlying the relations between variation in natality, growth of labor force, and growth of employment have been analyzed by R. A. Easterlin.

A labor force has three possible sources of growth: increase in the domestic population of working age, increase owing to net immigration, and increase in labor force participation as relatively more persons of a given age decide to become gainfully employed. Natural increase in the working-age population is an autonomous component, the product of forces controlling natality (say) 15 or more years earlier, whereas the other two sources are induced, reflecting economic and other factors that may prompt immigration as well as upswings in the relative numbers of people, by age, in search of jobs. When aggregate employment fails to keep pace with growth of the working-age population, unemployment on the part of young people newly entering the labor force will increase, especially if their number is relatively great because of a past upsurge in natality.

Even given echo effects of past variation in the G.R.R., the impact of variation in the number of new entries into the labor market may be cushioned in the absence of minimum wage laws, trade-union restraints, and so on. Variations in the entry rate of persons newly joining the labor force are predictable. Relative shortages can be met by drawing on retired workers, augmenting labor-force participation on the part of women, and temporarily increasing the number of hours worked per week.

4.6. PROBLEMS CONNECTED WITH OLDER PERSONS

In the past men were enjoined to honor their elders and heed their elders' wisdom. Moreover, elders generally resided near their descendants and were able to contribute to the conduct of the affairs of households, especially in agricultural settings. Even so, literature is replete with complaint of the hardness of old age, accompanied as it often was by poverty and misery. Yet until modern times, as I have indicated, the relative number of older persons was small. For example, with a G.R.R. of 2.5 to 3.0 and a life expectancy of 30 to 40 years, only 4 to 6 percent of a stable population would be over 59 years of age, and a much smaller fraction over 65. With a birth rate of 41.65 and natural increase rate of 5 per 1000, only about 4 percent of the population would be over 64. These percentages correspond very closely to those in Asia and South America around 1950 and the United States in the early nineteenth century, but they are lower than those in parts of Europe around 1850, which ranged from 4.64 in Great Britain to 6.47 in France, where natality had long been falling.

Today in the developed world the fraction of the population over 64 is much higher than it was in the past or than it is in underdeveloped countries. Given a life expectancy of around 75 and an increase rate of about 5 per 1000, nearly 15 percent of the male population would be over 64. This fraction is slightly above the 13.1 percent anticipated for Europe in the year 2000, and about one-fourth above the 10.6 percent found in 1965, when elsewhere the corresponding fraction ranged from 2.7 percent in Africa to 9.1 percent in Northern America. The fraction for the United States in 1965 approximated 9.6 percent and could exceed 10 percent by the close of the century. Indeed, should the American population become stationary, the fraction would eventually approximate 15 to 16 percent.

The major problem associated with increase in the relative number of older persons is that of so ordering society that older persons are not compulsorily excluded from gainful employment and effective participation in social and political activities. There need be no concern about the magnitude of per capita output, for, as I noted earlier, the ratio of persons of working age to the total population is at or near the maximum when a population is stationary or nearly so. Then potential average productivity is at or near the maximum. This potential will not be realized, however, if productive persons in upper age brackets are denied employment by government, trade unions, corporate bureaucracies, or choice-restricting institutional arrangements.

Prolongation of life at the individual level augments the number of years a person spends in retirement. His support in retirement comes largely from the rest of the community in most instances, since the implied productivity of his accumulated capital usually is small. His "right" to support is based upon pension and similar contractual and quasicontractual claims against the community; it may be increased through provisions by the state for assistance and income supplements. But income from all these sources usually amounts to not much more than half of what an individual received before retiring.

Such a situation is characteristic of advanced economies, especially the United States, but it is not characteristic of less developed economies. According to United Nations estimates life expectancy at age 15 for males in the early 1950s approximated 54.5 years in industrialized countries, 49.5 in semi-industrial countries, and 46.1 in agricultural countries. A smaller fraction of these years is spent in the labor force in the more advanced than in the less advanced countries; in industrialized countries 45.3 years are spent in the labor force and 9.2 years in what amounts to retirement, or roughly 5 active years for each year of retirement. The figures in semi-industrial countries are 43.1 and 6.4, or 6.7 active years for each year in retirement. In agricultural countries the inactive years number 4.6; active, 41.5, or 9 active years for each inactive year. Accordingly, while incomes are much lower in semi-industrial and agricultural countries than in industrial countries, the condition of the retired agricultural and semi-industrial worker may worsen less, in comparison with what it was when he was employed, than that of the industrial worker. The advantage in question, if it exists, is not very significant unless the retired worker enjoys the equivalent of social security or a small pension. This originates in the fact that life expectancy at (say) 60 or 65 is lower in the less developed countries; it will shrink as life expectancy expands.

A retired person is likely to suffer a second disadvantage in most countries—erosion of the purchasing power of his essentially fixed pension or similar claims through inflation. In the United States consumer prices rose about 3.75 percent per year between 1940 and 1970, and about 2.25 percent per year between 1950 and 1970, a period dominated by expanding, unproductive governmental expenditure. Suppose a person retires with the equivalent of an income equal to 0.7 of his income before he retired. At the end of 10 years, given a 25 percent increase in consumer prices, the retiree's real income would be about 53 percent of that on which he retired.

The situation of a retiree who derives his income from fixed-income securities or claims is suboptimal even when prices are stable. For even if a retiree's real income remained unchanged at 0.7 of what he made before retiring, he would experience a steady worsening of his relative fraction. Let's talk about retiree R and his nonretired associate C. Suppose both had relative incomes of 100 before R retired on a fixed income of 70. Suppose also that technical progress increases average income 2 percent per year, and that C experiences this increase, so that his real income at the end of 10 years is 122; then R's *relative income* is not 70, but 70/122, or 57, because R, on a fixed income, no longer shares in the fruits of technical progress since such progress is seldom reflected in falling prices. Either nonretirement or a combination of constant prices and a social credit for the aged can preserve the relative position of the older worker and allow him to share in the product of investment in education, science, and technology that is financed through public and eleemosynary funds and perhaps the source of growth of income per capita in the neighborhood of one percent per year. If the retiree does not share in the growth of output not imputable to private investment, his portion may be said to flow to the nonretired population.

The best guarantee of an older worker's security against inflation and of his receipt of income generated by nonprivate investment is to remain employed. Accordingly, the older worker's right to employment needs to be protected. It needs to be protected also because being employed helps to preserve an older worker's social status, for in the United States perhaps more than elsewhere enforced withdrawal of a person, especially a male, from the labor force tends to accentuate and accelerate his withdrawal from other forms of community-oriented socio-economic activity and thus often impairs his psychic or physical health.

For purposes of depicting what may be the prospective situation, let us hypothesize the case of a man with a life expectancy at birth of about 74 years. This implies the chances to be nearly 98 in 100 that a newly born male will survive to age 20 and (say) then enter the labor force. Once he is 20, and provided life expectancy remains unchanged, the chances are about 85 in 100 that he would attain the age of 65, at which time he could count on about 15.5 more years of life. Should mortality from all causes be reduced by about 30 percent, life expectancy at age 65 would increase to something like 16 years for males and 19 years for females. Under conditions such as these, should a male who enters the labor force at 20 retire at around 65 he would have worked about 45 years by the time he retired, or in the neighborhood of 2.8 to 3.0 years for each year he would expect to live in retirement. Should he retire at around age 55 after 30 years of work, he would spend about two years in retirement for each three at work. The question the prospective retiree faces therefore is this: Will he have been able by age 65 to accumulate enough claims to support himself and (probably) a wife over a period of 15 to 16 years for himself and around 19 years for his wife, or enough by age 55 to support himself and his wife in idleness for some 20 to 22 years?

Insurance of the security and comfort of older persons retiring from the labor force calls for three conditions. First, the ratio of the years spent in the labor force to the years likely to be spent in retirement must be kept high enough to enable an older person to retire on an adequate income, probably over 50 percent of his income when he was in the labor force. If the work-retirement ratio is too low, the older person's retirement income will be too low, or else he will have protected himself against this by living in austere discomfort while young and faced with heavy family expenditures; ten or fifteen years of saving between 50 (when supposedly family demands slacken) and 65 may prove inadequate. Second, the assets of retired persons must be guaranteed against erosion by inflation, which is largely the product of governmental mismanagement and the domination of economies by trade unions, oligopolies, and other antisocial coalitions. Third, retired persons deserve to share in the fruits of social progress traceable to governmental investment, which accounts for a considerable share of the increase in output per head. This might be accomplished by establishing a Social Credit for the Aged under which retired persons would have their real incomes increased by the state at a rate (say) of one percent per year, subject to upper limits on this claim. Under present conditions only those in the labor force or those drawing income from equities share in the fruits of progress. Of course if prices fell as output per head rose, the fruits of progress would automatically be distributed through increase in the purchasing power of money incomes.

4.7. THE FUTURE

The age composition of the population in the future will depend mainly upon fertility. Should it descend to the replacement level, the relative number of persons 45 or older will exceed that of persons 18 to 44. If, however, fertility remains high enough to permit an increase of close to one-half of one percent per year, the numerical advantage will pass to those aged 18 to 44 (see Table 4-1). The amount of political impact associated with changes in the age structure depends upon the degree to which political factors dominate economic factors, since economic power tends to grow with age in greater measure than political power.

Of greater concern here are two considerations, the nature of governmental policy and the degree to which morbidity is reduced and life at higher years prolonged. Inflation is likely in most countries under modern monetary conditions, given unwarranted faith in the unemployment-preventing role of rising aggregate monetary demand, together with trade-union ascendancy and the continuing multiplication of persons who are economically unemployable except at wages below those that are current. It will be essential, therefore, that the state guarantee the real value of pensions.

Should morbidity decline, life expectancy would increase somewhat and so would the fraction of the years between 50 and 80 that might be spent in the labor force, because a decline in morbidity tends to strengthen the resistance of the body to diseases that in time become fatal as well as to reduce the frequency of disability. Morbidity rises with age; it is much higher among those over 44 than among those 15 to 44. To what extent morbidity by age has declined in recent years in various parts of the world is not easily determinable, but in the United States it has declined slightly among females but not among males (indeed it has increased somewhat). Presumably man's environment, given increase in pollution, noise, and urbanization, is no longer so favorable to health in advanced countries as it used to be, though advances in medicine have offset this in some measure. Life expectancy among American females at age 65 (16.4 years in 1967) was exceeded only by that in the Netherlands, whereas that for males at age 65 (13) was exceeded in a number of countries, among them Bulgaria and East Germany.

Should this environment improve, however, and man's life expectancy at birth rise, life expectancy at age 70 will also rise, though not notably. Thus with female and male life expectancy at birth at 72.5 and 68.6 years, that at age 70 will be in the neighborhood of 11.4 and 10.2. With female and male life expectancy at birth at 77.5 and 73.9 that at 70 will rise only to about 12.6 and 11.2. Presumably, given reduced withdrawal from the labor force, then involvement in significant activities and greater engagement in participatorial recreation and less in spectatorial would tend to prolong life at advanced years.

In the most complex patterns of human behavior...underlying biological factors consequent upon the fact that man is first of all an animal play a role of the foremost rank of importance.

RAYMOND PEARL

As the above quotation suggests, the role of cost may not be highly visible to most members of a population, but a careful observer may see costs at work. In this chapter we examine the economic costs of population growth, the gross and net benefits associated with these costs, and human response to the incurrence of these costs. The term *economic costs* is restricted here to those outlays and effects that are translatable without difficulty into real monetary terms (though all costs, burdens, and so on, can be priced arbitrarily and thus reduced to monetary terms); various time and physiological costs are not included. A distinction needs to be made, however, between economic costs and benefits associated with *growth* of population and economic costs and benefits associated with a larger as compared with a smaller population. We shall not be concerned here with whether a larger population is preferable to a smaller one, or a growing one to one that is nearly stationary, because the answer to each turns on noneconomic as well as upon economic considerations. These questions are dealt with in Chapter 7.

CHAPTER FIVE

Population Growth: Costs, Benefits, Net Effects

We need to distinguish between objective costs and benefits and sub-jective costs and benefits. By objective costs and benefits we mean the values assigned by impartial observers to the burdens and the gains associated with a decision-maker's actions, such as those that have to do with the reproduction and rearing of a child. By subjective costs we mean the values assigned to these same burdens and gains by the respon-sible decision-maker—usually the *present value* of the anticipated costs and benefits. This distinction is necessary for several reasons. First, the course of action that a rational individual will pursue is determined by his subjective assessment of the gains and burdens likely to be associated with that course of action. He will be disposed to act in a certain way if his estimate of the gains exceeds his estimate of the losses sufficiently to offset any conscious uncertainties; otherwise he will be inclined not to act. Accordingly, if one is studying the behavior of individuals, it is subjective costs and gains that must be taken into account, even if they do not correlate highly with objectively assessed costs and gains. Over time, of course, if a decision-maker has opportunity to make a particular type of decision (such as whether to reproduce and rear another child) a number of times and experience the consequences, he will, if he was initially in error, revise his estimates of costs and benefits to make them correspond more closely with estimates that are based on his prior ex-perience of the gains and burdens.

Second, an assessment of gains and burdens by impartial observers serves at least two purposes. (1) It can determine whether a proposed course of action is likely to be beneficial from a community point of view and thereby provide guidance to policy-makers. (2) It establishes rough benchmarks in the light of which a potential decision-maker can revalue his subjective estimates. In the following discussion we are concerned mainly with costs and benefits that are objective in nature.

5.1. COSTS IN GENERAL

There are a number of cost-producing aspects to population growth that can be identified and described. Before we do this, however, we need to agree upon the meaning of costs in general. The production of any good or service has a cost: the materials, equipment, and human services, labor, and skill used up in the course of production. We call these materials and services *inputs.* Now we can define *production* as the transformation of inputs into output, into particular goods and services; the cost of output is the costs of the inputs of which it is com-posed. The production cost of anything therefore turns on the signifi-cance of the inputs—that is, on how useful they would be if they were otherwise employed. If the alternative uses of these inputs are insignificant, then that which is made out of them is relatively low in cost, and conversely. Outputs and inputs need to be conceived of as flows over time. Inputs are continually being transformed into output, the flow of which moves in the wake, so to speak, of the flow of inputs. Changing conditions may initially affect output and through it the flow of inputs, as they may initially modify the flow of inputs and thereby affect the resulting flow of output. Population growth can be viewed as a flow of output into which a flow of appropriate inputs is being transformed, accompanied all the while by a flow of waste.

Costs may be entirely incident upon the individual or organization that has occasioned them, or they may fall partly upon the responsible parties and partly upon others or upon the community at large. From a behavioral point of view this distinction is important. Let us divide costs C into C_i and C_e, where C_i is costs incident upon the individual or agent responsible for them and C_e refers to costs that fall not on this agent but upon others. Let O designate the output associated with C. Then the agent engaged in producing O will be governed only by C_i. Even though O is of less value than C (the sum of C_i and C_e), it pays the agent to produce O so long as O is greater than C_i since someone else will be bearing cost C_e. In modern society, unlike in a frontier society, a considerable fraction of the cost of population growth falls in the C_e category, on others than on the parents.

A distinction that parallels and overlaps this one is the distinction between visible and invisible costs. When costs are indirect or of slow gestation, they are likely to remain hidden from the uncritical eye. Costs that are visible tend to be compared with the benefits to which the incurrence of such costs supposedly gives rise. Costs that are not easily visible or that are seen only incompletely do not enter fully into the calculus of outlay and return. An economy can behave rationally only to the extent to which all costs are taken into account. Indicators of performance such as Gross or Net National Product can summarize accurately what is taking place only to the point that they allow for all costs, those seen easily and those seen with difficulty. Individuals can adapt their behavior with full rationality only to costs of which they are aware and to which they are free to respond as they choose.

5.2. COSTS OF POPULATION GROWTH

The cost of a given increment of population is that which must be given up in order that the increment may be brought into existence. At the family level this cost consists of what must be given up to bring one or more children into the world and support them until they become self-supporting. At the national level this cost consists of that which must be given up in order to maintain a positive rate of population growth.

Some of these costs are direct, some are indirect. For example, outlays upon capital, education, and so on, for *additions* to a nation's population are direct and closely associated with population growth. Other costs are indirect. For example, population growth can modify a country's age composition or the pressure of numbers on resources, and these effects can result in greater direct costs. Because a considerable fraction of the costs of population are indirect, these costs constitute less of a deterrent to population growth than they would if they were direct.

We must distinguish, with respect to population as with any other durable product, between gross and net costs. If year in and year out births equaled deaths, a nation's population would be stationary, its rate of growth zero. Mere maintenance and preservation would involve an annual replacement outlay. For example, if the death rate were 14 per 1000, a birth rate of 14 would be required to balance it. The replacement cost would then consist of the annual outlay necessary to secure this number of births and support those already born but not yet self-supporting. If, however, the birth rate were 24, a death rate of 14 would permit the population to grow one percent per year. The cost of population *growth* would consist in the outlays essential to secure this annual *increase* of one percent; the outlay upon the reproduction and rearing of the 14 per 1000 who offset deaths of 14 per 1000 would be a replacement cost.

In virtually all countries both *replacement* costs and *growth* costs have to be met, because in all or nearly all countries births exceed deaths in both the short run and the long run, and population is *growing*. Under most circumstances, therefore, population growth may have two effects: (1) it increases costs of the sort involved in population replacement, and (2) it may also entail costs that are distinct from replacement costs.

In a *dynamic* world both *replacement* and *growth* costs have a qualitative dimension. That part of the young population which is viewed as a *replacement* of those who die each year is not in practice distinguished from that part which is viewed as an *addition;* the members of the two groups are brought up together and in the same general way, in a way that usually entails improvement in the "quality" of the population. In practice, therefore, replacement amounts to more than merely keeping numbers and quality intact; it also involves outlays for *improvement* of the quality of those viewed as replacements comparable to the corresponding outlays upon those viewed as additions.

5.3. FORMS OF POPULATION-GROWTH COSTS

Now that we have discussed the general costs of population growth we shall examine them under eight headings: capital costs, age-structural costs, unemployment costs, environmental costs, density costs, costs in terms of freedom, conflict-producing costs, and qualitative costs. Some of these costs are associated closely with population growth as such, and others are associated with increase in population density. In the end, however, density costs are generally reducible to terms of growth costs, and so we do not distinguish between them sharply except to note that because of differences in density the costs of maintaining stationary populations may differ.

5.3.1. Capital Costs

As Harry Johnson points out, we need to view " 'capital' as including anything that yields a stream of income over time, and income as the product of capital." Capital then includes all inputs invested today in order to yield income tomorrow—inputs in equipment and construction, productive education and health, discipline and skill, training and re-training, and the accumulation of scientific knowledge and its conversion into applied knowledge; indeed, in everything embodied and dis-embodied that is tomorrow-facing. It we view capital this way, we can conceive of economic growth "as a process of accumulating capital in all [its] manifold forms" (Johnson), and we may correctly say that increase in potential productivity per capita and in income per capita is the result of increase in capital per head.

Capital as we have defined it is transformed into population, most of it usually for population replacement and the rest for additions to the existing population. Today's increment of population represents yester-day's collection of capital inputs. Its presence suggests that yesterday a choice was made to convert "capital" into additional population instead of into improvement of the material condition of the existing population and its replacement. Population growth thus may be purchased at the expense of improvement of the existing population. What is the purchase price?

We can only answer this question imprecisely, because the actual cost is a range that varies widely from country to country and within countries. In general, outlays per child within a country vary with the country's average income and with the socio-economic status of the family into which the child is born. In money terms it tends to rise commensu-rately with family income, because as a family's economic condition improves it spends more upon its children. In the United States, for example, a child spends about one-third more time in school than he needs to reach current levels of educational attainment. A family finds itself trapped in a culture complex that continually presses the average propensity to consume in most families toward unity, given that institutionalized provision has been made for the support of parents in their years of retirement. Accordingly, whatever the current direct cost of a given rate of natural increase, it tends to rise as average income rises, and the amount of inputs required to produce and equip a person for public and private life increases. An indirect cost—opportunities sacrificed—also rises because the earnings a mother foregoes to reproduce and rear children move up with average income.

Under the circumstances, estimating the cost of population growth for purposes of international comparison may proceed somewhat as follows, since it is very difficult to translate absolute costs in one country into absolute costs in another. We may suppose that it takes inputs worth about 4 percent of a nation's national income to provide material and services for *additions* to a stable population growing one percent per year, and to this amount we may add 2 percent to cover other capital and service outlay and to allow for the adverse effect of population growth upon a country's age composition. Then the cost to a nation of a one percent annual population growth rate would approximate 6 percent of a nation's annual income.

The total cost consists of the input of goods and services absorbed by the child as it passes through, say, the first 18 years of life and, upon its attainment of adulthood, of the industrial, public, and domestic capital required to equip the now mature child for full membership in the community. The input cost per person under, say, 19 bears a fairly definite relationship to a nation's average income, say one-half or more, while the cost of capital equipment approximates average reproducible tangible assets per head, usually in the neighborhood of four to five times average income. Some allowance must be made also for inputs lost through death, since only 98 percent or less of those born will reach age 20.

Most estimates of the cost of population growth relate to the costs of reproducing and rearing children. In the United States in 1968, tangible assets approximated $15,400 per capita, or 4.26 times national income; reproducible assets $11,820 per capita, 3.32 times national income. Accordingly, maintenance of the wealth/population ratio when population is growing one percent per year calls for savings of between 3.3 and 4.3 percent of national income. By comparison the cumulative input cost per child, exclusive of foregone earnings, probably falls within a $2 to $3 thousand per year range. For example, Dr. Jean L. Pennock of the U.S.

Department of Agriculture found the cost in 1969 dollars of raising a child through the first 18 years of life to range from $19,360 for a rural nonfarm child in the north central region to $25,000 for a rural nonfarm child in the West. Given equivalent levels of living, costs for rural farm, rural nonfarm, and urban families are similar in some regions, but vary somewhat in others. The estimated cost per child amounted to 15 to 17 percent of average disposable family income (which approximated 85 percent of national income). Of the total cost, the housing share was as high as 30 percent; food also absorbed as much as 30 percent in some areas; clothing and a residual category including recreation and personal care amounted to 10 to 12 percent each, while the transportation share was somewhat higher. Medical care ran only 4 to 6 percent and education only about one percent, since the state bears most of the direct cost of education. Aggregate cost per child rises with age; it is 75 to 90 percent higher in the eighteenth year than it is in the first year. These estimates may be contrasted with an estimate of $122,500 for raising a child to 18 in a New York City foster home in 1971 and a comparable estimate of $34,464 in a natural home.

In the mid-1930s the cost of bringing up a child to age 18 in families of five persons was $7766 when family income approximated $2500 per year, and $16,337 when it approximated $5,000–10,000 a year. The cost to society of all families considered together was about $100 higher; this addition allows for the fact that in the late 1930s about 6 percent of those born died before age 18. If allowance is made for the 172 percent increase in consumer prices by 1969, the costs for the two family-types in 1969 dollars according to the standards of 1935–1936 would be $21,124 and $44,437. This cost would be much easier to bear today, however, since per capita real disposable income is about 129 percent higher today than in the mid-1930s. It is not surprising, therefore, that actual outlays upon children have risen in response to this increase in family income and raised the standards of expenditure much above those of the 1930s.

Cost estimates such as Pennock's—$1100 to $1400 per year—do not include allowances for outlays made by the state and supported out of taxation, for the cost of equipping an individual with public, domestic, and industrial capital, particularly upon his attaining adulthood; neither do they allow for higher education which usually is pursued beyond the eighteenth year. If these additional costs were put at $1000–$2000 per year, the total cost per year to (say) age 21 would run $2100 to $3400.

Let us suppose that a stable population grows continuously 1 percent per year and that cost per child of a given age increases at the same rate as average income. The cost of this growth, we may infer from the cost estimates given in the preceding paragraph, would then run 5 to

8 percent of national income. These estimates include no allowance for the income a mother must forgo if raising children makes it necessary for her to give up employment.

This allowance for income forgone may approximate or exceed the direct cost of bearing, raising, and educating children. It enters into the total cost estimates potential parents make when deciding whether to have a child. This allowance or cost is mainly an overhead and hence does not increase in proportion to the number of children; the cost of an additional child may therefore be somewhat below the computed average cost of several or more children.

Population growth can slow down the growth rate of output per head (1) by absorbing capital that might have been employed in increasing output per head and (2) by shunting capital into less productive channels. (1) Suppose that average income and population each increase 1 percent annually and that the rate of population growth descends to zero. If a 1 percent rate of growth absorbed 6 percent of national income, the resources thereby represented might be available for investment, say at 10 percent, to yield 0.6 percent of national income; this 0.6 added to the rate of increase of 1 percent in average income would raise this rate to 1.6 percent per year. Were the process reversed, and the rate of population growth increased by one percentage point, the rate of growth of average income would fall about 0.6 percent. (2) We need also to take into account that returns on investment differ widely, in part because less technical progress is embodied in some forms of capital than in others, and in part because the yield on some forms of capital oriented to population growth (like housing) is likely to be relatively low. The extent to which the underlying population is affected by the incorporation of capital into population growth is conditioned by the use to which this capital might otherwise have been put. Had the use been increase in power to produce articles of mass consumption especially suited to the tastes of the underlying population, the effect of population growth would be more adverse than had the capital been used otherwise.

5.3.2. Age-Structural Costs

As I explained more fully in Chapter 4, a high rate of population growth gives rise to a less favorable age structure even when a population is stable in form. For example, given a G.R.R. of 2.0 and a life expectancy of 70.2 years at birth, the population would grow 2.33 percent per year and only 54.7 percent of the population would be 15 to 59 years of age. Given a G.R.R. of just over 1.0, however, this percentage would be about 58, 6 percent higher. Potential productivity per capita would therefore be about 6 percent higher. Furthermore, with a birth rate of about 14 instead of about 30 and a completed family size compatible with close to a zero rate of growth, a larger fraction of the female population would be free to enroll in the labor force.

5.3.3. Unemployment Costs

As we saw in Section 5.3.1, the rate at which capital is formed per head tends to be inversely related to the rate of population growth. Moreover, when the per capita rate of capital formation is relatively low, not all of an economy's capital requirements can be met, so some will be met less fully than others. This shortage will probably be especially incident upon employment-oriented investment, with the result that those factors of production or inputs complementary to labor will grow less rapidly than the labor force, or at least not fast enough to make something like "full employment" possible. Accordingly, the relative amount of unemployment, underemployment, and disguised unemployment will be high. This condition is most conspicuous, of course, in high-fertility underdeveloped countries.

5.3.4. Environmental Costs

The environmental costs of population growth assume two distinct forms: (1) those associated with the increasing pressure of numbers upon environment, and (2) those associated with dissipation of environment.

(1) Man's physical environment contains stocks of irreplaceable elements, among them appropriately situated space suitable for man's specific spatial needs. Such elements set limits to man's capacity to maintain an expanding standard of life, though such limits are not always felt in the short run, when relative abundance seems to rule. For example, the utilizable amount of land can be increased directly if exploitable land remains available, or the effects of its scarcity reduced through recourse to substitutes (fertilizer, water) for land. The stock of conventional energy sources may conceivably be augmented through recourse to fission and fusion and materials adapted thereto. Modern alchemy may substitute more abundant for less abundant natural resources. And so on. In the end, however, increase in the pressure of population upon man's physical environment generates problems whose solution absorbs inputs that might otherwise have been utilized to augment the flow of goods and services per capita or to make more free time available per capita.

(2) Destruction, uglification, and pollution of man's physical and ecological environment would not be entirely avoidable even in a stationary population, in part because infection from disease may be controllable only by pesticides that become pollutants. The processes are

accelerated, however, by growth both of population and gross consumption, by-products of which are waste, ash, and contaminants, together with air-borne and water-borne waste and, occasionally, thermal pollution. Air-borne wastes bring about deterioration of environments, especially of those where population is concentrated, while water-borne wastes pollute the soil and foster the growth of obstructive algae and water plants. Both types of pollutants, because they foster the growth of some forms of organic life at the same time as they check that of others, alter the composition of the organic world. Climates might even be changed, through the introduction of excessive amounts of carbon dioxide into the atmosphere. Stewart Udall has described the outcome in terms reminiscent of John Stuart Mill's observations 125 years ago: "We live in a land of vanishing beauty, of increasing ugliness, of shrinking open space, and of an overall environment that is diminished daily by pollution, noise, and blight." Much of this deterioration can be averted, but it will be increasingly difficult as numbers increase and become concentrated.

The order of magnitude of pollution costs alone is suggested by two recent estimates. A survey by the *U.S. News and World Report* (Aug. 17, 1970) put at about $26 billion a year the cost imposed on the United States by water and air pollution. Brewbaker reports that careful estimates put the cost of correcting environmental pollution in the United States between 1970 and 1975 at about 1.6 percent of Gross National Product. According to Lave and Seskin, the reduction of air pollution by half in major cities would greatly reduce certain types of disease and related mortality and thus save at least $2 billion a year in costs currently associated with morbidity and mortality.

Pollutants, contaminants, and solid waste are borne away over three types of channels: water, air, and man-made vehicles; the demands on these channels are exceeding their capacity. Overloading water and air with heat and contaminants can befoul even distant areas, whereas overloads of solid waste befoul only the vicinity of the source, or the places to which men carry it. Overloaded water and air, moreover, can change the character of environment in greater measure than can carriers of solid wastes. The burden of solid waste is increasing, however. It is estimated that in the United States refuse collected per capita in urban areas, put at 2.75 pounds per day in 1920, will reach 8 pounds per day by 1980, and an increasing share of this will be stuff that is noncorrodible and not easy to reuse within urban centers. Already in 1969 solid wastes produced in the United States amounted to about 20 pounds per person, of which only about three-quarters was removed; and the removal burden will continue to increase. In general, whatever the origin of the water-, air-, or land-borne wastes and contaminants, given *ceteris paribus,* their volume will tend to grow roughly in the measure that Py increases, where P denotes population and y designates average income.

In at least one respect, however, population growth is more conducive to pollution than is increase in GNP per head, or affluence as such. Increase in affluence does not intensify use or compel extension of exploitation of the environment in the same degree as increase in population does. Accordingly, since the ratio of waste to output increases as exploitation is extended in response to population growth, aggregate waste in need of removal necessarily outstrips population growth even when average income remains unchanged. Population growth will intensify man's demands upon atmospheric and aquatic conveyors of pollutants at least in proportion to the growth of numbers and probably in greater measure. It also intensifies pollution at the hands of poultry and livestock, the husbanding of which becomes highly concentrated.

5.3.5. Density Costs

Some costs associated with population density increase generally as numbers grow and specifically as the growth process, often stochastic in character, concentrates an increasingly large fraction of the urban population in large cities. Most costs are associated with metropolitan and megalopolitan growth, of which aggregate population growth is a necessary though not a sufficient condition. Thus, increases in temperature, contaminants, and noise come in the wake of population concentration. Various costs tend to be intensified by population concentration and increases in man's mobility (which augment the pressure each individual generates as well as that of which he is conscious). We shall return to this matter later in this chapter.

Increase in population density may conduce to greater economic inequality unless it is counterbalanced by the system of taxation. The rent of land and similarly nonaugmentable factors of production will tend to rise. The returns to other agents complementary to labor may also rise. Beyond some level of density, therefore, the pretax distribution of income will tend to be less favorable to labor than when population is less dense, given no change in other conditions.

5.3.6. Costs in Terms of Freedom

As population increases and density contacts among individuals multiply (usually at a much faster rate than the population increases), one likely result is an increase in people's struggle for power over each other and a decrease in joint activities designed to augment man's control over his physical environment. Another result is an increase in demand for collectivistic controls over the life and activities of man. Some of these, like property rights, are essential to peace and prosperity, but others may be facilitated by gross ignorance of consequences or by ideological dislike of market and pricing mechanisms. The eventual upshot of such collectivistic trends is the separation of ruled from ruler and possibly the development of garrison-like states run by bureaucracies little subject to control by the underlying population. Population growth accelerates this centralizing tendency and the resulting diminution of man's individual liberties.

5.3.7. Conflict-Producing Costs

Population growth may affect international relations in three ways. (1) If it unduly augments its outflow of exports, it can worsen a country's terms of trade. (2) Under certain circumstances it can intensify the totality of conditions making for war. (3) It can generate frustrations and social unrest in the underdeveloped world that spill over into the international realm. Population growth is not now likely to produce any of these effects in the United States, but it can do so elsewhere in ways that would affect the United States. Population growth is thus essentially a catalyzer rather than a major causative agent.

5.3.8. Qualitative Costs

Adverse selection tends to be a concomitant of excessive family size and of dysgenesis made possible by reduction of child mortality. Negative euthenic and eugenic selection has other causes besides a relatively high rate of population growth, but a nation's capacity to deal with adverse selection of any origin is greater when its rate of population growth is low.

5.4. THE COSTS OF POPULATION DENSITY

Overall population density needs to be distinguished from localized density—urban, metropolitan, etc.—touched upon in Section 5.3. Such a distinction makes the costs of overall density resolvable into costs associated with a population's being larger rather than smaller—that is, with the pressure of numbers on the ensemble of natural resources and man-made equipment at the population's disposal. Costs associated with this increase in pressure are of two sorts (described in Chapter 2 or noted earlier in this chapter). First, utility-yielding instruments that were free when numbers were smaller now have taken on the ·character of economic goods, since people now want more units than are available. Furthermore, because the best of these units have been brought into full use, it has become necessary to resort to inferior units. In other words, it has become necessary to exploit inferior components of the physical environment, with the result that the marginal cost of exploitation tends to rise or, given technological improvements, is greater than it otherwise would be. Second, the rate of using up depletable natural resources is increased, given continuation of some level of per capita consumption, because a larger population means more consumers. There is a third set of costs that is the product of intensified human interaction, especially when density passes threshold levels, but these are treated later in connection with population concentration.

One of the models devised by demographers to describe in skeletal form the forces at work is the logistic. This model postulates that the rate of natural increase varies inversely with population density. It decreases because supposedly the combined force of increase in mortality and/or decline in natality under a given set of conditions reduces the relative number of living persons that a growing population can continue to add to itself. This process continues until a population becomes stationary. The process itself may be said to reflect the increases in costs that are associated with increase in population density, that decrease the Gross Reproduction Rate, and that augment mortality under given conditions. This process is more evident in the demographic behavior of animal and insect populations than in human populations, however, because humans may modify underlying conditions and thus in effect delay the operation of the process or diminish the rate of decrease in the rate of natural increase associated with increase in population density.

5.5. COUNTERVAILLANTS TO POPULATION GROWTH AND DENSITY

There are economic advantages that may be associated with both population growth and increase in population density that partly or completely offset at least some of the costs. Under some circumstances these advantages can be so great that a larger rather than a smaller population is preferable. We are not concerned here with what we call *an optimum population,* because determination of the optimum is based upon economic and noneconomic considerations and possible trade-offs between the two. The supposedly countervailing effects are of diverse sorts.

1. The most important countervailing effect is *specialization,* what Adam Smith called division of labor. As growth of population and average income enlarge the extent of the market for goods and services,

specialization may be intensified and its advantages multiplied. Perhaps the greatest manifestation of increase in these advantages was that which accompanied the supersedure of a predominantly agricultural economy by one predominantly industrial in character. Once the process is completed, however, many if not all of the advantages of specialization tend to be exhausted, because the scope for specialization within the service sector of modern economies may be limited and international exchange may have given release to most economies of specialization. Furthermore, increase in the gross economic efficiency attendant upon increase in specialization is accompanied by increase in costs associated with this specialization until the increment in efficiency is outweighed by the accompanying increment in costs. In short, while some economists believe that increase in aggregate output is still accompanied by increase in returns, there is strong evidence that increments in aggregate output can be wholly traced to increments in inputs.

2. A corollary to the argument that increasing returns accompany population growth is the belief that the burden per capita of overhead costs—governmental and related supposedly lumpy inputs—falls as population increases. This tendency, if it exists at all, exists only in small states and even then may be offset by accompanying costs.

3. Malthus and others have assumed that population growth is essential if man is to bestir himself and overcome his "natural" inertia. Associated with this assumption is the belief that necessity is sufficiently the mother of invention to more than offset any disadvantages attendant upon the population growth that initiated the inventive activity. This argument is of doubtful validity under most conditions.

4. Population growth, it is said, enlarges markets and thus frees overly optimistic entrepreneurs of the costs of overcapacitation associated with unwarranted overinvestment in particular lines of enterprise. This argument overlooks the fact that investment planners usually attempt to take into account all relevant considerations, among them population growth, and so any propensity to err in forecasting market expansion is not likely to be affected significantly by the rate of population growth.

A companion argument—that population growth makes easier the absorption of innovation into an economy—may be somewhat more tenable, because such growth in numbers and hence demand may act more speedily than release of purchasing power based upon increase in average real income to provide employment for workers displaced by innovation. The outcome in any concrete situation depends, however, on demand elasticities and other relevant circumstances.

5. It is sometimes argued (1) that technical progress is the product of "geniuses"; (2) that the number of "geniuses" is a linear function of

population size; and (3) that the increase in this number tends at least to counterbalance the adverse effects of more people. This argument overlooks that only some geniuses are likely to contribute to economic progress and that their contributions tend to be much less important than what Josiah Stamp called "a mass attack of high talent."

5.6. THE RESPONSE OF HUMAN FERTILITY

The factors and conditions that determine human fertility are numerous even when fertility has been brought under a high degree of control. Population growth and increase in population density bring stimuli to bear upon those of reproductive age; these stimuli may be arbitrarily described as economic in character and others as noneconomic in character, even though no definite basis exists for distinguishing between economic and noneconomic motives. Since noneconomic disadvantages associated with producing children can often be overcome through expenditure upon means calculated either to eliminate them or to compensate parents that suffer them, noneconomic disadvantages can sometimes be expressed in terms of monetary cost.

In order to see the impact an increase in numbers and population size might have upon fertility, it is essential to relate the demand D for children to variables that may be affected directly or indirectly over time by growth of population size. Let us therefore write

$$D = f(y, p, t, w, e, v)$$

Here y is average income, p the structure of prices, w a measure representing the utility parents expect of children, t economic tastes or preferences, v noneconomic values that might or do condition D, and e the expensiveness of children.

Not much need be said about w, since change in their value probably is largely independent of increase in numbers as such. The utility parents expect to derive from children—w—is of three forms: (1) affection and other satisfactions, (2) the income and other assistance that children can contribute to the operation or support of the household and related enterprises, and (3) the economic security, love, affection, and moral support parents expect to have from children in time of distress and retirement. Today the amount of utility to be had from (2) is much smaller than formerly: most children contribute little if anything to the support of their household. The utility to be had from (3) remains important, though much less so than formerly because increase in population density has made it possible to institutionalize the provision of economic support—though not of affection and moral support—in old age. Moreover, inflation can reduce institutionalized support and thus make older persons somewhat dependent economically on their children. The utility expected of children is generally much less now than it was even a few decades ago, and so the value of w is less than before, though affection continues to be prized.

The value of e depends mainly on the socio-economic status of the parents, together with the propensity of parents to spend on children. Since increase in population density intensifies interpersonal communication, it has probably contributed to increase in the value of e. As a result D has been reduced somewhat.

With p, t, and v assumed to be independent of y and hence given, increase in y tends to increase D and hence the level of fertility within the population of reproductive age. Of greater importance even than the level of y are the expectations of a population concerning the subsequent behavior of y. If it is expected to rise steadily and considerably, fertility will probably be stimulated in greater measure than if little or no increase is anticipated. It is possible, of course, that expectation of increase in y will produce an offsetting change in t, with the result that an increase in y, or in the anticipated degree of upward movement in y in the near future, has no influence on D.

It is common, of course, for the changes that elevate y also to influence t, because increase in y is mainly a result of investment in science, technology, or physical equipment, much of which brings new products and services into existence and thereby changes taste t accordingly. It is possible for v to be affected indirectly by changes in the wake of investment in ways that are sometimes favorable and sometimes unfavorable to fertility and hence to D.

For the reasons indicated, it is not possible to predict how fertility will respond to increase in y, though undoubtedly an actual or anticipated decrease in y would tend to reduce D. This tendency is strengthened when increase in unemployment is the cause of the decline in y (as during the downturn of the trade cycle), especially if unemployment benefits are not provided by the state and proportioned to family size.

It may be argued that the forces that have served to increase y over time have also served in the long run to modify both t and y sufficiently to offset or more than offset the fertility-stimulating influence of increase in y. These forces affected the response of D to y indirectly as well, since decrease in infant and child mortality tended to be associated with increase in y and to diminish the number of births required to produce a desired number of sons and daughters aged (say) 10 to 15 or older.

Whatever the level of y and its prospective growth, the significance of y for most categories of a population depends upon p, the structure of prices. When goods and services dominant in the family budgets of the mass of population decline in price more than goods in general, fertility tends to be stimulated. This change in the structures of prices amounts to an additional increase in y expressed in real terms. A change in p of the opposite sort will produce a converse effect. As we noted earlier, a good deal of investment has been directed to reducing the relative prices of goods favored by those of reproductive age.

This trend can, however, affect D and hence fertility indirectly in the longer run, because if goods and services preferred by the masses become relatively cheap in relation to y, changes in t and possibly even in v may take place as y increases. It may come to be accepted that other types of goods are now within reach of the purse of those who could not earlier entertain the new tastes. If this be true, demands of families upon their average income y will increase and end up by depressing family size.

Demand for children, D, can be influenced by government expenditure patterns that augment y in real terms. Taxation that reduces y tends to affect fertility adversely. If, however, the manner in which tax revenue is expended reduces the private cost of children to families, the effect may be equivalent to an increase in y, subject to the condition that realizing this increase turns on having children.

The changes in p to which fertility and D are most sensitive are those in the price of goods and services consumed in large amounts by children—housing, food, health-oriented products, and so on. If the prices of these goods rise relative to y and to prices in general, fertility will be depressed, because then real income is reduced and goods and services not oriented to children are priced relatively low and so attract customers who might otherwise have invested in reproduction.

The demands for some goods and services, being complementary, are highly intercorrelated. It may happen, therefore, that reduction of a certain price or prices will produce a chain reaction. The cheapening of the motor car had this effect (in far greater measure than did the cheapening of the seventeenth-century stagecoach), giving rise to related "needs" and providing access to many goods and services, with the result that in the end the products that were centered about the car absorbed a much larger fraction of y than the car purchaser had anticipated. A possible effect is a decline in D. Had the motor car remained higher in price relative to y, it would not have been purchased and there would have been no chain reaction.

Until now we have not looked directly at the utility of children—that is, at the advantages that parents *expect* to derive from the affection of children and in virtue of which they desire children. Changes in t or v can come about in such ways as to modify this source of utility. Strengthening this source tends to increase D to a point, beyond which additional children reduce utility per child and eventually in the aggregate.

We have assumed here that most potential parents rationally anticipate, with varying accuracy and uncertainty, the consequences of having children. It may be assumed, therefore, that an increase in the monetary and related costs of children relative to y would tend to depress fertility, and a decrease in these costs to elevate it. Experience may, however, modify the degree of response on the part of parents to these cost changes should they learn by experience. For example, disappointment at the initial consequences flowing from having a child or two could modify parental decisions about whether to have a second or higher-order child; a favorable experience would produce an opposite effect. Should the rate at which prospective parents discount the future increase markedly, the effect might be to diminish the present value of the utility expected of children and thus reduce the value of D and fertility. Increasing uncertainty about the future may have a similar effect unless children come to be viewed as a source of security in an uncertain world.

We have made only passing reference to genetic selection, a process that operates much more slowly than euthenic selection. It is evident that some individuals are much more tolerant than others of population pressure, crowdedness, and pollution. Since this tolerance is genetically conditioned, it is likely that genetic selection in metropolitan areas will favor persons disposed to such tolerance. We shall refer again to some of these matters in Chapter 9.

In earlier chapters, especially 3 and 5,
we dealt with topics that in this chapter
we shall examine from a different point
of view. We dealt with population growth and
some of its effects, and we touched
lightly upon the population capacity of some
parts of the world. We did not deal
carefully with the most fundamental
demographic question: How many persons
should a particular country or region support?
We cannot give explicit answers to this
question, but we can identify some of the
factors to take into consideration. In this
chapter we shall deal with questions of scale.

The scale Thompson refers to in the
above epigraph is that of living organisms, not
that of social organizations. In this chapter
we shall be concerned with the size of
social organizations—of nation-states and cities
in particular. The proper size of a social
organization is likely to be more responsive
to changes in the organization's
environment than is the proper size of
a living organism, but a living organism is
much more likely to suffer destruction

CHAPTER SIX   if its size gets out of balance with its environment

Population Optima

than is a social organization. There is much greater variance about mean size in the universe of social organizations—firms, cities, nation-states— than in that of living species, for reasons we shall discuss shortly.

Most of our discussion will relate to the scale of the nation-state, though later in this chapter we shall devote some attention to urban and regional scale problems and to factors that determine the optimum sizes for city and regional populations.

We shall not consider the matter of what constitutes an optimum rate of population growth, but it is to be taken for granted that a zero growth rate is indicated when a country's population is as large as desirable, and that if further growth of population is believed to be advantageous the rate of growth should not be too high. One might argue, for example, that such a rate not exceed one percent per year, because if the rate exceeds one percent too much of a country's savings will be diverted from improving the condition of the population to increasing its numbers. Moreover, the population will include more young dependents than are desirable, with the result that per capita productivity will be kept lower than it need be and the educational burden may be higher than the country can meet. We have ample evidence of the disadvantages associated with unduly high growth rates in many underdeveloped countries where incomes are low and efforts to increase them are both limited and handicapped by these high rates. For example, as we saw in Chapter 2, a high rate of natural increase, especially in rural areas, slows down the rate at which the urban fraction of the population can be increased as it must if economic development is to be carried forward rapidly.

6.1. POPULATION SIZE, STATE SIZE, AND AVERAGE INCOME

States can be too small or too large on political as well as economic grounds. In times past it was not essential that a state be large in size in order to realize such economies of scale as were to be had. Ancient writers (Aristotle, Plato) believed that small city-states (say of 100,000 or less) would be adequate on economic and political grounds, but the sizes favored seem to have been too small, even under these conditions, but then all the large empires, formed as they were of a number of dissimilar but relatively stable small units, collapsed in time and broke up into more stable components. Undoubtedly they were too large, given the systems of communications and government of the times, and the heterogeneity of the components. These political disadvantages were not swamped by the economic advantages associated with empire even though, as in the heyday of an empire such as the Roman, the resulting security and the prevalence of a single system of law reinforced those economic advantages associated with nonlocal commerce. We shall return later to whether the primary limit to the desirable size of a state is economic or political in character.

Over time, and particularly in the course of the past 200 years, economies both of scale and of agglomeration have increased. Until recently, at least, the course of invention has been such, on the whole, as to shift advantages in production to larger-scale plants and undertakings. It is true that some small plants have performed as well as some large plants, but mostly the economic advantage has been with larger states. This advantage has been accentuated by the freedom of large states from trade barriers of the sort encountered by small states beyond their borders. The trend in advantages of size has been associated with increase in the concentration of populations associated at least in part with advantages of propinquity in economic undertakings and with the manner in which transport has developed. Underlying both trends has been the course and application of invention, both characterized by efforts to reduce costs and produce new goods and services. Had effort been directed also to reducing optimum plant size it is likely that tendencies toward increase in plant and firm size and toward concentration of activities in space would have been less pronounced.

How large a population need a state have in order to realize economies of scale? The minimum has been put at 50 million. The findings of a symposium dealing with this question have been summarized by E. A. G. Robinson:

It is not going too far, perhaps, to say that it seemed to be our general impression that most of the major industrial economies of scale could be achieved by a relatively high-income nation of 50 million; that nations of 10–15 million were probably too small to get the technical economies available; that the industrial economies of scale beyond a size of 50 millions were mainly those that derive from a change in the character of competition and specialization—a change which may, if one relies on the contrasts between American and other experience, be explained partly by scale, but may also be attributed to differences of national outlook and to differences in the legal handling of the problems of monopoly, as well as to differences consequent on income and expenditure per head, and due, in part at least, to a richer endowment of natural resources.

Robinson goes on to argue that increase in size is not likely to give rise to *economic* penalties:

It may be open to argument whether the economies of scale to be achieved by integrating a number of nations, already of the order of 50 million in population, are great. There are probably significant economies of integrating nations of the size of 10–15 million. But in neither case is there any danger of loss of efficiency by doing so, if the larger nations that emerge conduct their affairs with equal efficiency. There are no possibilities of diseconomies of scale arising from the excessive size of the market. There are no penalties for being bigger than the minimum size, if such there be, that will exhaust economies of scale, provided that a centralized economic policy is not collectively more protectionist against the outside world or slower at making the adjustments of economic policy that will keep the parts of the integrated unit consciously operating at a high level of production.

If we contrast these statements with conditions in the world at large we may infer several things: (1) population density varies considerably from state to state among those large and wealthy enough to realize all or most economies of scale; (2) international trade, together with other conditions, enables the economies of some smaller states to perform as well as those with 50 million or more; (3) most of the world's states are too small ever to realize all economies of scale; (4) some large states with low incomes could become capable of realizing all economies of scale if they reduced their rates of population growth to zero and devoted the savings to increasing average output and income.

These inferences are supported by a cursory survey of 127 states for which the *World Bank Atlas* provides information. Of the 14 states with a population of 50 million or more, in 1968 only seven averaged close to $1000 or more Gross National Product per capita, and these ranged in density from 29 to 710 inhabitants per square mile. Of the 25 states with close to $1000 or more Gross National Product per capita, 17 numbered 20 million or fewer (Israel, with 2.7 million, was the smallest). International trade contributed importantly to the capacity of small countries to cope with their smallness by importing products or inputs not economically available at home and exporting enough of some products to permit specialization despite the smallness of the domestic market for some of the specialties. Of the 127 countries for which output data are given for 1968, 72 numbered less than 10 million and only 30 numbered over 20 million. Of these 127, 81 averaged less than $500 Gross National Product per capita and of these 48 averaged $200 or less.

The absence of a significant relation between size or density of a country's population and its Gross National Product per capita does not mean that these population factors are without influence upon per capita product. Many circumstances affect the level of output, often sufficiently to swamp the influence of population factors. The most important conditions that account for a relatively high level of average output—say a Gross National Product of $900 per head—are the overall levels of industrial culture and technology. These began spreading from the United Kingdom and Western Europe nearly two centuries ago, but up to now they have only spread to and through a few countries; as recently as 1968 only 26 countries averaged $900 or more Gross National Product—18 in Europe and six in Europe Overseas (Australia, New Zealand, Northern America, and two countries adjacent to Northern America). Only Japan lies outside the sphere of European civilization, whence it adopted Western technology, and income in the other two (Libya and Venezuela) is so high because of petroleum. Spread of this technology to and through countries that average $200 or less Gross National Product—countries where close to 2 billion people live—is currently limited by many conditions, among them high rates of population growth, which absorb 5 to 10 percent or more of Gross National Product and retard development in a number of ways.

Three inferences may be drawn from this review. First, it is unlikely that many of the world's small states will ever become large enough, through commercial or other integration with similar or larger states, to realize economies of scale in the absence of considerable international trade. Second, in a world dependent upon thermonuclear power and ancillary apparatus, very few countries are describable as politico-military powers. Military considerations cannot therefore enter significantly into the population policy of many countries. By contrast, in the nineteenth century and even more in earlier centuries military and related uses of manpower received considerable attention. Third, since countries differ in so many respects, international comparisons yield but limited information about potentially suitable population policy for any particular country; each country needs to take its own situation and particularities into account.

6.2. MAXIMIZATION

Optimization consists in maximizing or minimizing some variable quantity; its mathematical theory goes back to Leibniz, Euler, and others, its conception to ancient times. Political and economic writers at various times had crude notions of the optimal size of political organizations. Best known is Plato's conception of the city-state, or *polis*, which he put at 5040 citizens—by implication about 60,000 inhabitants—a number apparently associated with something like the maximum attainable value for the social welfare index that Plato had in mind.

Plato's and Aristotle's conceptions were not suited to the age of empire that came to the Mediterranean world with the ascendancies of Alexander and later of the Romans. During and after the Middle Ages in

Europe one finds reference both to manifestations of localized population pressure and to the alleged need for more people, which need was increasingly stressed as nation-states emerged and labor came to be regarded as the main source of both products and military power. At least as early as the eighteenth century, however, economics writers recognized that numbers tended to be excessive for economies based predominantly upon agriculture, that a country's population needed to be held in check since maximum population meant that there was only bare subsistence for the bulk of the population. It followed that for every country there was a population of optimum size, given which a people would be about as well off as possible. To this J. S. Mill gave most effective expression when, in 1848, he pointed out that no gain was to be had from further population growth in countries such as England, that their numbers were already sufficient to exploit division of labor as fully as was desirable, that although improvements in methods of production would continue effective application of them would not therefore require larger populations, and that if population were stationary incomes could rise and living conditions steadily improve.

Mill's view was essentially valid, but the problem is more complicated than he represented it. In 1848 industrialization was under way, but conditions of life for the common man were usually unattractive and the beauty of the countryside was already threatened. For purposes of exposition let us select I to represent a social welfare index to be maximized. With I at a maximum, each member of a nation-state is about as well off as he can expect to be under the circumstances governing the value of I. Whatever be this value, it is functionally related to many variables, of which population is but one. We may therefore write

$$I = f(P, Y, d, t, g, R, T, p, V_1, V_2, \ldots V_n)$$

where P is size of population, Y aggregate income, d its distribution, t external trading relations, g the weight accorded suppositious concerns of future generations by the current generation in arriving at decisions, R a country's stock of natural resources, T the character of its technology, p the pattern of tastes of population P, and V_1, V_2, V_n other variables by which I is influenced directly or indirectly. In sum, I has many determinants, of which population P is only one.

The fundamental question here is: What effect does any change in the variables governing I have upon the magnitude of P that is required to maximize I? Let's begin with a situation in which I is at a maximum, which means that P may be described as of optimum size. Changes in other variables will have one of three effects upon the optimum magnitude of P: they may be without effect, they may increase it, or they may decrease it. Most of the change in I is associated with changes in other variables than P. As a result the adverse effect of increase in P may be hidden, in a dynamic society, by the I-increasing influence of changes in variables other than P. This has usually been true in the past, but it may cease to be true when better measures of costs and benefits are developed.

The variable determinants of I are roughly of two sorts. Most of them —especially t, R, and T—affect the capacity of the economy to supply the final bill of goods, services, options, and so forth, included in I. Several of them, however, affect the content of I, which is an aggregate indicator of the structure of a society's wants; this is especially true of g and p, and somewhat true of d. Change in d affects the composition of aggregate demand much as does change in g, which reflects the impact of change in the importance attached to future versus present generations. Change in p reflects the relative amount of utility attached to children, and change in this can modify the optimum value of P.

Of the variables that determine the size of the population optimum for a country under given conditions, the most important are p, the population's tastes or preferences, R, its natural resources, T, the state of its arts or technology, t, its international trade, and the degree (if any) to which the economy remains subject to economically realizable increasing returns.

A people's tastes are important because they determine the input content of the bill of goods and services of which I is the indicator. The input content of I in turn implies a relatively large or small optimum population under given conditions, since inputs vary most noticeably in terms of real cost. For example, if the products entering into a population's standard of life are predominantly labor embodying, the magnitude of the optimum population will be larger than if these products were predominantly natural-resource embodying. If the utility attached to population and hence to inputs incorporated in population is high, the optimum will be larger than when this is not the case. Accordingly, given emphasis upon the utility of population or upon a labor-oriented standard of life, retardatory and limiting factors will become operative less rapidly.

Increases in I and in the magnitude of a country's population, be it of optimum size or not, are limited ultimately by R, T, and, in lesser measure, g, which determines the extent to which the amount and character of contemporary consumption are restricted so as to provide future generations with a more salubrious environment and a more extensive R than might otherwise be available to them. As I explained in Chapters 3 and 5, improvements in T may augment the fraction of man's finite physical environment, which he can make subservient to his uses and to his capacity to economize in the use of R, by reducing the input of R per unit of final output and by recycling—that is, by increasing the number of times inputs of R may be used before they become economically nonutilizable.

We may view R as a component of a nation's stock of capital and hence subject to the rule that the capital of the economy be kept intact, and that any loss of value through physical use or dissipation be replaced with an equivalent source of value. Such replacement of R presents problems not associated with ordinary "capital" equipment, which consists largely in human labor and skill; because R is made up of components (such as petroleum) that either are subject to depletion and waste or, though not depletable, are essentially fixed in physical supply. It is only through T, therefore, that the utilizable aggregate of R can be kept abreast of the effective aggregate demand for R. Accordingly, given limitations to increase in the capacity of improvements in T to augment the utilizable aggregate of R, R sets limits to the size both of population optima and of sustainable maximum populations. International trade t may overcome shortages of R in particular countries, but usually only temporarily if the world stock of relevant and potentially utilizable resources is fixed. Such trade may, of course, reduce the population capacity of the countries exporting depletable forms of R unless the returns from this trade are used to transform their economies. Some sources of R (for example Kuwait) are, of course, devoid of political potential and will pass from the economic scene with the exhaustion of their exportable natural resources.

We have been treating R as if it were a set of actual and potential inputs that are interchangeable and hence essentially homogeneous, but we must allow for the fact that

$$R = \Sigma R_1 + R_2 + \ldots R_n.$$

These several subsets of R cannot always be substituted for each other. Moreover, they differ markedly in their relative scarcity and replaceability. Accordingly, limitations on the growth of output and on the magnitude of optimum population size depend upon the indispensable components of R rather than upon R as an aggregate. The relative scarcity of these components depends, of course, on the composition of output—that is, on the kinds of goods and services that enter into the standard of living and the indicator I. Relative scarcity is subject to modification, therefore, through change in consumption patterns, decreases in the use of relatively scarce components, and increases in the use of relatively abundant components.

If we ignore limitations imposed by R and temporarily identify I with average output or Y/P, we may define the optimum population as that size of population that gives full release to increasing returns, to the tendency (if present) of aggregate output of goods and services to increase faster than an *optimally constituted* aggregate of inputs entering into this output. Sources of increasing return are to be found mainly at the level of producing plants, possibly at the firm level, and in the degree to which it is possible to operate all plants at the minimum-cost level of output—that is, at the optimum level of *interplant fit*. While agglomeration of economic activities also makes for economy within limits, it is the result of the distribution of activities in space rather than of population size. When there are increasing returns, overall output per overall unit of input generally rises.

It is at the level of the plant (or what amounts to a plant) that the sources of increasing return—differentiable from return attributable to technological progress—are most readily distinguished. Private and public activities can be translated almost entirely into terms of plants (that is, isolatable systems of activities) that interlock, through the medium of the price system or analogous administrative and coordinating structures, with other and complementary systems. This lets us describe most economies that are usually described as external to plants or as varying with size of firm as internal to plants or their equivalents.

Plant size may be expressed either in terms of output or of input, but the most useful index of size for purposes of location or optimum population theory is that of manpower employed. This index has been affected by invention, innovation, and the comparative prices of inputs, especially labor and capital. In the past the trend in plant size was upward, but it could be downward, particularly if miniaturization of plant size or economy in the use of labor became an objective.

We can say that interplant fit is optimum when all plants are of optimum size and operate at minimum real cost per unit of output, in which case both final consumer goods and intermediate products are forthcoming at minimum cost. The size of the population associated with minimization of unit cost varies directly with minimum optimum plant size, level of consumption, and variety of output; increase in any of these tends to increase the number of consumers and producers with whom something like an optimum interplant fit is associated. The advantage of optimum interplant fit is less when the variable cost curve is quite elastic and variable cost rises slowly.

We can divide the countries of the world into three categories. (1) In a few countries of considerable geographical extent and limited population (Canada, Australia) a population of optimum size is still attainable.

In these an increase in P may, within limits, contribute to an increase in I. (2) Some countries of considerable geographical extent are already so heavily populated that an increase in P is a source of disadvantage, though I remains subject to increase through improvement in other variables. India, Pakistan, China, and Japan are cases in point. (3) Many countries are too small in geographical extent and population to accommodate an economy of optimum size as described in Section 6.1. Some of these countries are already so densely populated that any increase in P is disadvantageous to increase in I. Others may experience increase in I as a result of increase in P, but only within limits. Either way countries in this category are heavily dependent upon international trade; they stand to gain from technological changes that reduce optimum plant size.

As we noted earlier the concept of optimization applies to the distribution of population and to economic activities in space within countries. It applies also to the distribution of births among families, in that some distributions give rise to populations superior in quality to those produced by other distributions. We shall examine these two applications of the concept of optimization in Chapter 8. All population policies are most useful when they are based on concepts of optima set in the framework of a system.

6.3. WHETHER MAXIMIZATION TAKES PLACE AUTOMATICALLY

Fertility (hence population growth rate) and the size of a country's population are conditioned by many factors, all of which bear upon actual and potential parents. Some factors make for the restriction of fertility; others conduce to it. It may be said, therefore, that a population exists in a universe of penalties and rewards that condition fertility. Fertility tends to change both with the incidence of these penalties and rewards upon various sections of a population and with change in a population's capacity to control fertility. Given a sought value of I, it may become a concern of public policy, should the universe of penalties and rewards not conduce adequately to the realization of I. To this issue we shall turn in chapter 8.

Let us suppose, however, that there exists some population for which, given the appropriate values for relevant variables, the indicator I is at a maximum. Let us call this population the Optimum and label it O. Then if we let m denote the degree of population maladjustment, and A the actual population, we may (as did Hugh Dalton) write

$$m = (A/O) - 1.$$

If A is greater than O and m is positive, there is overpopulation; if A is less than O and m is negative, the population is too small. There is zero maladjustment if A equals O.

Does m tend to approximate zero? Does the rate of natural increase tend to rise when m is negative, and fall when m is positive? There appears to be little or no such response. Throughout much of man's demographic history A has been greater than O; population responded upward to improvement in economic and related conditions, but was halted in time by increase in mortality, sometimes associated with increase in m. For the propensity to increase is very great, as we noted in Chapter 1; thus with a life expectancy of only around 25 and a Gross Reproduction Rate of slightly over 2.5 (one not uncommon today and in the past), a population will double in less than four centuries. With a higher life expectancy the rate of increase is higher. Up to now, therefore, in all countries and above all in the least developed countries, population has grown. In terms of the above formula A has continued to increase, often at an increasing rate, and usually much faster than O; as a result m has continued to increase even when the maximum population capacity of countries has increased.

The failure of an increase in m to affect the growth of A significantly is traceable to the absence of sensitive feedback mechanisms running either from m directly to actual and potential families or directly to agencies of the state and thence indirectly to families and to formulators of immigration policy. This insensitivity has several sources. From m or increase in m there flows little stimulus that many perceive as unfavorable to the realization of their material or other expectations. This insensitivity is increased by the long interval between initiating steps to reduce fertility and their impact upon the determinants of I and hence upon I. Benefits in the form of losses averted and gains realized are slow to emerge. So also is any conduct-determining awareness of these advantages, even though the slowness with which natural increase falls makes adjustment of the economy to the advent of a stationary population easier. Insensitivity to change in m is accentuated by the fact that an increase in I frequently accompanies an increase in m because improvements in other determinants more than offset the adverse effects of increase in P. Only response to immigration in immigrant-receiving countries is likely to be associated with sensitivity to m, mainly on the part of members of certain groups such as trade unions to what they perceive as adverse effects of m or of increase in m, (such as increase in competition from immigrants). This response can, however, result in a curb upon A and m only if immigration is brought under control by the state. In view of the absence of widespread sensitivity on the part of actual and potential families to m, response on the part of a population to m or to increase in m turns largely upon the degree of intervention by the state, and any such action is likely to be taken only if the state is prompted thereto by influential groups sensitive to m.

6.4. POPULATION SIZE AND OPTIONS

As I indicated in Sections 6.2 and 6.3, very few countries are in a position to achieve a population of optimum size, and the only choice confronting those countries that are is between halting population growth and not halting it. Nor is the range of choice much greater for countries with populations below or in the neighborhood of optimum size, because even if fertility declines and the Net Reproduction Rate descends to 1.0 in the near future the populations of most countries that experience such a decline will continue to grow for perhaps 50 to 70 or more years, so that by the time these populations do become stationary they will be 30 to 40 or more percent larger than at the time their true rates of natural increase fell to zero. The populations of most of these countries will probably exceed optimum size.

In Sections 6.2 and 6.3 we neglected the difficulties associated with defining I satisfactorily and the implications of these difficulties for the formulation and execution of policy. It has been implied that I defines the "welfare" of a population such that the content and distribution of "welfare" are generally approved by the population as constituting an end to be sought. In reality, of course, there is no consensus—let alone universal approval or acquiescence—on any welfare function. It is not possible, therefore, to define I in such a way that the underlying population will generally behave compatibly with it, nor can I be translated into any policy that makes highly probable its realization however it is defined.

Because of the difficulties described and of diversity of opinion respecting what should be included in I, an alternative approach may be preferable. With each population size P_i a set of options, O_i, and a corresponding set of costs, C_i, may be associated. Most of these options will be exercised, at least in the initial base period, but those that relate to the future may or may not be exercised. Let us suppose a series of options, $O_1, O_2, \ldots, O_n$, a sequence of populations, $P_1, P_2, \ldots, P_n$, and a corresponding *explicit* cost with each set of options, $C_1, C_2, \ldots, C_n$. If population grows—P_1 increases to P_2—option set O_2 will replace set O_1 and cost C_1 will be succeeded by C_2. Implicit costs are also reflected in the content of two sets of options; for, while O_2 will largely intersect with O_1, O_2 will include options not included in O_1 and exclude options included in O_1. The options included in O_1 but not in O_2 have been displaced by increase in population from P_1 to P_2 and by such changes as distinguish the economy at time period 2 from that at time period 1. Options included in O_2 but not in O_1 have been made possible by these same changes in P and technology. The loss of options included in O_1 represents an implicit cost of the increase in population, together with accompanying changes, but whether this loss is significant turns on the degree to which tastes and preferences have changed to eliminate desire for the omitted options.

Comparison of O_2 with O_1 raises several questions. Is it possible to ascertain through opinion surveys whether O_2 is preferable to O_1? Would it be possible to obtain all or most of the additional options included in O_2 even in the absence of an increase in population from P_1 to P_2? Could the probable content of O_2 have been closely enough estimated in time period 1 to permit comparison of O_2 with O_1 and determination of whether increase in population to P_2 was essential or desirable? Even if comparison of O_1 and O_2, or of O_2 and O_3, were feasible, it is questionable whether O_1 could be compared in time period 1 with a somewhat imaginary and uncertain O_6. Short of state intervention, however, it is not likely that comparison of O_2 with O_1 at time 1 would prevent increase of P_1 to P_2. Even so, it is thinking in terms of optima, systems of optima, and options that makes for improvement and realization of policy objectives.

6.5. WHETHER LARGER POPULATION IS DESIRABLE

The question we must continually answer is whether the probable advantages (if any) associated with increase in population outweigh the disadvantages. If this question is continually asked, a people will become alert to both the real input costs and the implicit costs in terms of options sacrificed that are associated with the replacement of a smaller by a larger population. Moreover, continually posing this question will develop alertness to the impact of population increase.

The most important decisions in life are the irreversible ones, the adverse effects of which are not remediable, or are remediable only at great cost. Of the decisions that are most irreversible, demographic ones, together with their side effects, are most significant. For this reason augmentation of a population or city calls for careful consideration of the effects. When sizes in the neighborhood of an optimum are nearly as attractive, the smallest is generally to be preferred, because it makes the smallest demands on fixed and depletable resources and it imposes a smaller quantum of irreversible costs.

Presumably in the future there will be sharper distinction made between *growth* of population and *replacement* of (say) a smaller by a larger population. This distinction bears not only on differences between the impact of growth of population and that of differences in population size, but also on distribution of births among families, a dimension of significance in respect of the utility attached to children. The average number of children per woman in a stationary population—2.11—is lower than in a growing population, with the result that the fraction of the women bearing five children or more must be lower.

It should be easy in advanced economies to bring population growth to a halt; for if they resemble the United States, elimination of unwanted births would bring the number of children to the replacement level, 2.11. In contrast births in underdeveloped countries, most of which presumably are wanted, greatly exceed the replacement average, which means that even if a larger population is not wanted numbers will continue to grow.

6.6. SPATIAL OPTIMA

In this chapter we have devoted our attention almost exclusively to national optimum population size. The concept of optimum applies equally to the distribution of population in space, to regional populations, and to city size. These matters are discussed in other chapters. Here we need only note that market forces alone are unlikely to yield optima, because the costs and benefits associated with population increments, say to a city, are seldom distributed similarly. Hence growth is governed by the relation between private costs and private benefits instead of that between social costs and social benefits. Collective intervention is essential therefore if we are to keep social costs and social benefits—that is, *all* relevant costs and benefits—in balance, to prevent excessive growth of population concentrations, and to secure the most preferred distribution of population in space.

In Chapter 6 we defined population
optima, and indicated that because the
physical environment accessible to any
national or similar group of people is
finite, achievement and maintenance of a
population of optimum size implies
a stationary population, one with a zero
rate of growth. Reduction of a
population's growth rate to zero does not,
however, imply a static economy, for
average output may continue to grow. In
this chapter we are mainly concerned
with the economics of a stationary
population. After a brief examination of
earlier populations we shall compare it
with a growing population.

7.1. A BACKWARD GLANCE

A rapid rate of change destroys
perspective. Ours is an age that extols
change and development and makes
of something called "growth" a primary
political objective, a Juggernaut empowered
to override all concerns and values
in its way. Emphasis on growth and change
began in the eighteenth century; it
greatly increased in the nineteenth

CHAPTER SEVEN century when, as A. N. Whitehead observed,

A Stationary
Versus a Growing Population

"the method of invention" was invented and broke "up the foundations of the old civilization." So great did Western man's consciousness of change become that by the early twentieth century some were questioning, not change as such, but whether the current rate of change imposed unnecessarily high costs. Now such questioning is widespread, above all in the growing number of endorsements of a zero rate of population growth and in efforts to curb the costs of industrial growth.

Secular change has been absent from virtually all of mankind's career. Man has lived in a steady-state economy throughout most of his literate history; to put it more accurately, he has lived in a static state subject to great perturbations originating in periodic pestilence, destructive wars, redistributions of power, and the economic instability that often comes in the wake of war and pestilence. He has long had the power to increase his numbers and income, but he did not do so. For example a Gross Reproduction Rate of 2.5 (common in underdeveloped countries) would have permitted his numbers to double in roughly a century, even with a life expectancy of only 30. Yet as we noted earlier the world's population grew very little in the first millenium of the Christian era and at a very low rate over the next 500 years. Nor did average output rise significantly. Indeed, not until during and after the seventeenth century did the world's rate of population growth rise, to around 20 percent per century. Average output, still very low, also begin to rise perceptibly. The Western world was moving out of an essentially static state into one that was dynamic and would become increasingly so.

The main reason for the very slow growth of man's numbers and average income has been his capacity to frustrate the propensity of social (and other) organisms to grow exponentially for sustained periods of time. For example, if average income had risen 5 percent every 50 years, it would have been about 5.25 times higher in 1700 than it was at the beginning of the Christian era. So also would population, had it grown at this rate. Had both grown at these rates, aggregate output in 1700 would have been about 25 times higher than during the time of Caesar Augustus.

The underlying reason for the lack of substantial growth prior to the eighteenth or even early nineteenth century was the unproductive use of economic surpluses, generation of which is almost inevitable in all but the most primitive economies. Such surpluses were in effect appropriated and used unproductively by the rulers and kept classes of the nongrowing nations. As Richard Cantillon noted around 1730, "the Fancies, the Fashions, and the Modes of Living of the Prince, and especially of the Landowners, determine the use to which land is put in a state." Later Adam Smith described average output as depending upon the fraction of the population of working age "employed in useful labor." With the growth and spread of the bourgeoisie, initially manifest in the medieval town, larger fractions of the surplus were invested productively; this tendency was accentuated by the growth of Atlantic-facing commercial centers and oceanic trade. As a result, what had been an essentially static steady-state economy gave way to a nonsteady-state dynamic one, with the increasing application of science and technology in agriculture and industry.

Such dynamic states first appeared in the European sphere of civilization, mainly in Western Europe. The economies of Asia had slowly approached the upper limits of the technological systems underlying them. Later on, of course, in the nineteenth and twentieth centuries, the technologico-economic systems of Western Europe spread eastward in Europe and across the oceans and eventually set in motion economic and demographic upward movements there.

Technological and medical progress, which has greatly increased populations during the past two centuries and may enable them to increase another 100 to 200 percent within a century, has also facilitated rapid reduction of the rate of population growth. The newer modes of contraception, together with abortion, entail little pain cost to the users, with the result that when they are easily available they tend to be adopted rapidly, once small families are seen to be preferable. In the past achieving a small-family system entailed greater costs. Indeed, in the past high mortality rather than low natality has mainly been responsible for stationary populations. It is to be expected, therefore, that populations will first approach stationary states in those countries that can be described as advanced.

7.2. THE ADVENT OF A STATIONARY POPULATION

The advent of a stationary population requires two kinds of accommodation on the part of population and economy: accommodation to the *approach* of a stationary demographic state and accommodation to a stationary demographic state as such. Let's first consider the approach, but suppose it to be gradual and hence free of significant disturbance of the age structure.

Let us define Y', the growth rate of Net National Product or National Income Y, as follows:

$$Y' = P' + a'$$

where P' is the growth rate of population P (a fixed fraction f of which is in the labor force L), and a' is the growth rate of output per capita a (f times the growth rate of output per member of the labor force). If we abstract from increasing returns, the probability of which is zero or close to zero in the United States (particularly if one allows for *all* costs of population growth), Y' will approximate a' if P' descends to zero. Given *ceteris paribus*, however, the decline of P' to zero, together with slow change in age composition, may increase a'.

Whether this happens depends upon the degree to which shrinkage of *widening* investment (investment in population growth) is replaced by *deepening* investment (investment per capita). Suppose P' declines from one to zero percent. Then the aggregate of inputs C invested in this one-percent-per-year rate of population growth becomes available for investment in "capital" per head (that is, C divided by P) at the current rate of return r on new investment. Should all of C be so invested, a will be increased by rC divided by P. If under these conditions C approximates .05Y and r approximates 0.1, Y increases by .005Y, and a by half a percentage point above its initial level k (say 2 percent per year), that is, from k to k plus the addition of rC divided by P equals 2.5 percent. Of course, should a portion of the released inputs C be devoted to leisure instead of to production, a' will increase by less than half a percentage point. We may say that in an advanced economy a decline of one percentage point in the rate of population growth will generally result in a decline of something like three-fourths to one-half of a percentage point in the growth rate of aggregate income or output. In an under-developed economy, however, as Coale and Hoover have found, a decline in the rate of population growth may tend to increase the growth rate of aggregate output.

Should we include nonphysical investment in C, it may approximate 0.1Y, with the result that rC divided by P equals 0.01, and $k + 1 = 3.0$ percent; then the one percentage point decline in P does not lead to a decline in Y'. Improvement in age composition, which we discuss below, could prevent any decline in Y'.

Although the advent of a stationary population does not end aggregate economic growth, it can reduce the rate of aggregate economic growth and it will modify the composition of output. For with P' at zero, aggregate growth can cease either because growth rate S' of aggregate supply S declines to zero or because increase rate D' in aggregate demand D descends to zero. Also, S' could in the end descend to zero, given the inability of man and his societal apparatus to overcome the finiteness of the physical environment upon which he is dependent and to which he has access. Such inability is highly improbable, but it is possible that man will not find it worth while to exercise his capacity to continue S'

at a positive level. It thus becomes essential to examine the behavior of D'.

Let us therefore turn to the behavior of D, and write

$$D' = P' + ey'$$

Here D', P', and y' denote, respectively, the growth rates of aggregate demand D, population P, and average income y; e denotes income elasticity of demand, or the response of consumer demand to increase in y. If P' is reduced to zero, D' depends upon y' and e. Given that y' corresponds to a', which was described earlier and which by supposition remains positive, e becomes the strategic variable. The value of e for categories of commodities or services can exceed 1.0, but not when D' denotes the rate of growth of aggregate demand inclusive of *all* goods and services. In high-income countries e may be falling or on the verge of falling even though the level of y at which such decline is at hand has risen over time. Not only does *earning* income impose a cost in terms of *time*—of *leisure* foregone—and thus tend to hold down a' and hence y'; consumption itself also imposes costs. Consumption of any particular good or service takes time and thus restricts the remaining alternatives open to the consumer, among them enjoyment of sheer *leisure*. Consumption of some goods and services may also draw heavily upon a consumer's energy or endanger his health and thus limit his consumption of alternatives, among them enjoyment of *leisure* time. Inevitably, therefore, *time* and *physical* costs limit both the consumption and the production of goods and services; they slow down a' not only directly but also indirectly, by reducing the value of e below unity.

It is not expected that e will decline to zero, but it would be possible, even in a sybaritic society, for it to do so. The possibility of such an outcome is conditioned mainly, *ceteris paribus*, by the rate of increase in the variety of products, by circumstances governing the time and physiological costs of consumption, and by the level and rate of increase of y (which corresponds to average output a). Decline in the value of e is conditioned also by what happens to man's tastes or preferences and by the extent to which he resists the efforts of sellers to increase his wants and of producers to accelerate the obsolescence of the goods and services he purchases. Ironically, when producers develop goods that make great demand upon consumer time, such as television, they reduce the value of e. Decline of e is conditioned finally by the degree to which men develop a taste for collective goods, public and otherwise, and a capacity to supply them, since demand for these is susceptible of considerable growth.

It is to be noted that e as here used is little more than a mental artifact introduced to allow for the fact that, with population stationary, D' may not equal y'. Because D is an aggregate quantity it consists not only of the direct demand for consumer goods and services but also of indirect demands ranging from those for consumer durables to those for so-called higher-order goods whose services enter into lower-order goods as inputs. The demand for these higher-order goods is subject to greater fluctuation, therefore, than that for consumer services; it reflects the relationships described by the so-called acceleration principle. Thus a small relative increase or decrease in the demand for housing, or in the rate of increase in this demand, may produce a greater relative increase in the demand for components of the "industry" producing housing. The connections between lower- and higher-order goods and services merely complicate but do not modify the impact of growing demand for leisure upon growth of demand for goods and services.

7.3. ZERO VERSUS POSITIVE POPULATION GROWTH AND INCOME

A population that is not growing differs from one that is growing in two economically significant respects: (1) the *process* of population growth, which includes both *growth* and *replacement,* is superseded by a process of sheer population replacement; and (2) the *size* of the population ceases to increase. While the age structures of the two populations also differ, our concern in this section is with the economic significance of (1) and (2); the impact of changes in age structure I shall deal with in Section 7.4.

Associated with effect (1) is increase in the amount of mobile resources per head at the disposition of the stationary population, together with the consequent increase in that society's options. We have already described this outcome in Section 7.2. A comparison of saving and investment in a stationary population with that in a stable one that grows at one percent per year indicates that in the former potential physical investment per capita will be decidedly higher (50 percent) if investment amounts to 10 percent of national income in a growing population. Because as we noted earlier, a one-percent rate of population growth will absorb something like 5 percent of national income, which would be available for investment if a population were not growing. It is possible also that this investment will flow into somewhat more productive channels, because population-oriented investment such as housing is less productive than alternative forms.

Also associated with (1) is the release of at least some of the resources currently devoted to the education, training, and so on of increments to a population where it is growing. These resources can be used to improve the quality of a stationary population, or for other purposes.

Should trade-cycle tendencies be weaker in a stationary than in a growing population, average output and investment would be somewhat higher. These tendencies could become weaker to the extent that they are associated with *irregularities* in private and public expenditures upon durable wealth or physical capital, because the relative importance of expenditure upon all forms of physical capital will tend to decline, since relatively less demand is likely to be generated for structures and equipment of the sort highly correlated with *growth* of population and *internal migration* consequent upon such growth. This expenditure will also be less variable. Should the greater saving potential result in greater savings, interest rates would trend downward, which would supply some stimulus to investment but not greater variability. As we shall note, however, some economists fear that a stationary population is apt to oversave and thus produce underemployment.

Let's turn now to (2), the cessation of increase in the pressure of numbers on resources consequent upon the increase in population each year from a current P to a P plus ΔP a year hence. As a result, less of the growing stock of capital will be required merely to counterbalance increase in the pressure of an economy upon those components of the natural environment that are in fixed supply and nonaugmentable (such as space and hydropower resources) or depletable over time (minerals). For, though growth of average income and consumption will continue to add to this pressure, it will no longer be augmented by increase in the number of consumers.

Increase in environmental pollution and degradation will proceed at a lower rate, as will the need for investment in measures designed to cushion their incidence. Increase in pollution and environmental degradation will not end, of course, because it is caused by growth of average income and consumption as well as by population growth. Under similar conditions, however, an increase of one percent per year in average income and expenditure may give rise to less pollution and environmental degradation than will a one percent per year increase in population. The impact of increase in average consumption may also be reduced if cessation of population growth makes possible reductions in population concentration.

All this may be put in more general terms. Let's define π, the rate of increase in aggregate pressure upon the fixed and the depletable components of the environment of concern to man, as approximately

$$\pi' = P' + ba'$$

Here again P' is the growth rate of stable population P, and a' the growth rate of average output a; b is a multiplier described below. We may suppose that *ceteris paribus*, if ba' had a value of zero, π' would approximate P' unless increasing concentration of population caused π to grow slightly more rapidly than P. The relation of π to a is variable. With the value of P set at zero, π could increase faster or slower than a. Here b is a multiplier designed to translate the impact upon π of a one percent increase in a into terms of the impact of a one percent increase in P. If b equals one, the impact of a one percent increase in P is equivalent to a one percent increase in a. If b is greater than one, as in countries undergoing rapid industrialisation, a given relative increase in a intensifies π more than does an equivalent relative increase in P. But if an economy is in a stage in which services preponderate, b is likely to be less than one and to decline further. In an economy in which services preponderate, π will already be at a high level, carried there by past growth of both P and a; indeed, under some conditions increase in π will correspond to increase in Pa. Optimum distribution of a country's population will tend to reduce the value of π associated with a given value of P. Similarly, the value of π associated with a given value of a will depend upon the composition of a.

A decline of P' from (say) one percent to zero will reduce the value of π', but by less than one percent, because as I brought out earlier, decline in P' makes for increase in a', and this in turn increases the contribution of increase in a to increase in π. As a rule the net effect of a decline in P' will be a decline in π'.

7.4. AGE STRUCTURE AND INCOME

The age structure of a stationary population is at least as favorable to average productivity as the age structure of a growing population. By way of illustration we may turn again to the age structures of five male and five female stable populations in Table 4-1. The assumed life expectancy at birth is 71.2 years for males and 75 years for females. These life expectancies are combined with Gross Reproduction Rates that give rise to true rates of natural increase ranging from −5 per 1000 to 15 per 1000. The resulting stable-population age structures are in the table. The age structures for male and female populations with zero rates of growth are in the two columns headed zero (0). The columns of male age proportions indicate that the relative number of persons under 20 rises significantly with the postulated true rate of natural increase; the relative number in age group 20 to 24 rises slightly, and the fraction 70 years and over falls.

Three sets of figures stand out. First, the fraction of the male population within the productive age group (20–64) is higher when a population is stationary than when it is growing (57.95 percent instead of 56.56 percent or less). While the fraction is slightly higher when the rate of population growth is slightly negative, the discussion that follows is confined to a population the age structure of which is associated with a zero rate of growth.

Second, the relative number of persons of dependent age is higher in a growing than in a stationary population. If we include in this category those over 69, those under 15, and one-half of those 15 to 19, male persons of dependent age number 33.68 percent when this population is stationary and 37.61 percent when it is growing one percent per year. If we also include those aged 65 to 69 the corresponding percentages are 38.64 and 41.2. Older dependents are relatively more numerous in a stationary than in a growing population, but not enough to offset differences in the relative number of younger dependents.

The magnitude of the fraction of population 55 or older that is dependent is a product of institutional definition. Consider two male stable populations, one stationary and the other growing one percent annually, each with a life expectancy of 58.84 years. Suppose also that all aged 20 to 54 are in the labor force and that all males aged 55 to 64 are capable of working but are excluded from the labor force by retirement rules. In this stationary population males aged 20 to 54 and 55 to 64 constitute 47.97 and 10.64 percent respectively of the male population; in the growing population, 46.25 and 8.13 percent. Accordingly, if those aged 55 to 64 are enrolled in the labor force, its size is increased about 22 and 17 percent, respectively, in the two populations. Should the population that is growing one percent annually cease to grow, its labor force—those aged 20 to 54—will cease to grow one percent a year. Then, given expansion of the aggregate demand for labor, there will be concern lest cessation of population growth bring about a "shortage" of labor. Yet if retirement restrictions are removed, the stock of labor can be increased about one-fifth. If the sum of this increment and increase in the employment of females does not suffice, elevation of the wage level will serve to bring the demand for labor in balance with the supposedly fixed stock of labor. This hypothetical situation is similar to the case of Japan today: a retirement age of 55, a net reproduction rate slightly below 1.0 since 1956, and claims of labor shortages.

It is sometimes said that there will be fewer geniuses in a stationary than in a growing population because the age structure in the former is less genius oriented. This argument is not very tenable. The fraction of a population falling within the creative age group is about as high when the rate of population growth is zero as when it is higher. For example, if we suppose the index of males of potentially creative age to correspond to half of those aged 20 to 24 and 0.7 of those aged 25 to 44, the index value for a stationary population is 22.1 while that for a population growing 1.5 percent per year is 22.5. Furthermore, when a population is stationary more resources will be available for the development of potential geniuses. Finally, it is the world pool of developed genius that is important, since the products of this pool may be drawn on freely by all countries.

It has also been argued that too much responsibility for decision-making passes into the hands of older persons when a population is stationary, and that the result will be an unduly conservative gerontocracy with too short a planning-time horizon. This argument also is not very tenable. There is little difference in the relative number of males aged 25 to 44. It is true that, of those in a stationary male population aged 45 to 74, 26.9 percent are aged 65 to 74 compared with a percentage of 23.4 in a population growing one percent annually. It is easy, however, to prevent too much concentration of decision-making power in the hands of older persons by setting limits upon the fraction of administrative posts that persons over 60 or over 64 can hold.

It has also been argued that a relatively high rate of population growth is conducive to technological progress because then the number of persons in the younger and supposedly more progressive age groups is relatively large. These younger persons, it is assumed, resemble machines of recent vintage, in that they embody the latest and most advanced in scientific knowledge and technological skill. Moreover, they look with favor upon change since they anticipate many years of life in the course of which they expect to reap the fruits of change. By contrast persons in their late 40s and 50s can look forward to but a few years of possible gain from change. Furthermore, older persons, more imbedded in the socio-economic structure than younger persons, are likely to suffer greater cost from the impact of change.

Argument along such lines is of limited empirical validity, even given that older persons find change more painful than do younger persons. Consider three male stable populations, with a life expectancy of 71.2 years and growing, respectively, zero, one, and 2 percent. The ratio of the population aged 15 to 34 to those aged 35 to 64 is 0.7 in the stationary population, 0.9 in that growing one percent, and 1.14 in that growing 2 percent. If one selects instead as index of youth those aged 25 to 34, these ratios become, respectively, 0.35, 0.43, and 0.51. The weight of youth clearly is greater in the more rapidly growing populations, but this is partially offset by the fact that educational opportunity and capital formation per head are lower in the growing populations. Thus if we measure the availability of education by the ratio of the population aged 25 to 64 to those aged 5 to 24 we obtain 1.91 in the stationary male population and 1.43 and 1.06 in those growing one and two percent. Given these ratios, differences in capacity for investment, and the institutionalized character of the production of scientific and technological progress, only limited weight can be given to the argument that a "young" population is decidedly more progressive.

7.5. AGE STRUCTURE AND FLEXIBILITY

An economy may be described as consisting in a set of distinguishable sectors s_i numbered 1, 2, . . . , n, among which labor force L is distributed. Then total output (T) is

$$T = L_1 V_1 + L_2 V_2 + \ldots + L_n V_n$$

Here L_1 denotes the labor force attached to sector s_1, L_2 that attached to sector s_2, and so on; V_1 denotes output per member of the labor force L_1, V_2 that per member of L_2, and so on. Should outputs V_1, V_2, etc., increase we may denote the rates of increase by V'_1, V'_2, etc. We assume L to be stationary since the population (P) is stationary, and for the present the ratio L/P is assumed not to vary. We then have a *static* state if V_1, V_2, etc., are constant. We have a *steady* state *if* V_1, V_2, . . . , V_n grow at the same rate— that is, V'_1 equals V'_2 equals. . .V'_n–and demand for the output of each sector grows at the same rate as output in that sector. Under these conditions no intersectoral migration of labor and other factors would be required.

Actually, neither a steady state nor a static state is likely to emerge even though P and L are stationary. (1) Technological progress and investment vary from sector to sector, with the result that $L_1 V_1$, $L_2 V_2$, and so on, grow at different rates. (2) Demand for product also varies from sector to sector, according to the elasticity of demand for finished goods and services, as do the derived demands for the inputs that ultimately enter into consumer goods and services. There will be variation as well in the substitutability of factors for one another within and between sectors.

Under the conditions given, considerable intersector mobility of labor and other agents of production becomes essential to the maintenance of optimum economic equilibrium. It is in order to inquire, therefore, whether maintenance of such equilibrium is as easy in a stationary population as in one that is growing.

Maintenance of this equilibrium is conditioned by the ratio of the mobile labor reserve m to the total labor force L. This mobile labor reserve is made up of two components—n, the aggregate natural increase (if any) in the labor force L within the yearly interval 0-1, and w, replacements in the labor force of those removed in year 0-1 by death or retirement (age, disability, or any other cause). m equals n plus w in a growing population; in a stationary population m equals w, with a constant labor force L and a constant annual wastage equal to w. Accordingly, m divided by L is smaller in a stationary than in a growing population.

For illustrative purposes we can draw again on the United Nations study we referred to in Chapter 4. Given a male life expectancy of 70, a Gross Reproduction Rate ($G.R.R.$) of 2, and a representative set of labor-force participation rates, the rate of entry in a labor force per 1000 males is 33.7, 22 in excess of the withdrawals (6.2 retirees and 5.6 decedents). But with $G.R.R.$ at 1 the rate of entry is 19.2 compared with a withdrawal of 21.1 (12.1 retirees, 9 decedents). In a stationary population with $G.R.R.$ slightly above 1, the rate of entry will balance the rate of withdrawal in the neighborhood of 20, or about two-fifths below the rate of entry when $G.R.R.$ is at 2. The significant question is whether enough of these 20 are available for intersectoral transfer and the maintenance of optimum intersectoral balance under dynamic conditions.

We may generalize by dividing the sectors s_i of an economy into sectors s_j, each of which requires more labor in year 1 than in year 0, and sectors s_d ($s_i - s_j$), which require less labor in year 1 than in year 0. If i_d is the fraction of wastage w_d in sectors s_d that apparently needs to be replaced, then in a stationary population with a stationary labor force there will be $(1 - i_d)\Sigma w_d$ *new* entries into the labor force available for recruitment into expanding sectors s_j. Let the required increment in the aggregate labor force employed in sectors s_j equal $i_j \Sigma w_j$, where i_j is equal to or greater or less than one. What we have called the mobile labor reserve m, here equal to total wastage Σw_i, will be adequate so long as $i_j \Sigma w_j$ does not exceed $(1 - i_d)\Sigma w_d$. Should $i_j \Sigma w_j$ exceed $(1 - i_d)\Sigma w_d$, a combination of rising wages in sectors s_j and some emerging unemployment in sectors s_d (caused by some shifts in consumer demand from s_d products to s_j products) will stimulate intersectoral migration from s_d to s_j sectors. Had the labor force been growing by an increment n, the labor not theretofore employed and hence available to expanding sectors s_j would have approximated

$$(i - i_d)\Sigma w_d + n$$

and this sum would have met the growing labor force requirements of sectors s_j. There would therefore have been less upward pressure against wage levels in sectors s_j. Upward pressure will be diminished somewhat as more women enter the labor force, as age of retirement is moved upward (see Section 7.4 above), and as other circumstances increase labor-force participation. But there are limits to all these sources.

The experience of Australia during the past two decades supports this argument. Australia, with a policy of selective immigration, draws roughly half its increase in population from abroad. When a labor shortage develops, the immigration authority often is able to recruit immigrants with the required skills. As a result any upward pressure against the wage level is prevented, and the job vacancies are filled at the going rates for the skill and occupational levels in question.

Maintenance of intersectoral balance will be somewhat more difficult when the population and the labor force are stationary than when they are growing, and there will be more upward pressure against wage and price levels, particularly if an economy is dominated by interest groups interested in impeding intersectoral movement of agents of production and thus reducing the flexibility and capacity of an economy to adjust rapidly to changes in population or in the structure of demand or supply.

It is inferable that upward pressure against wage and price levels will be intensified as the rate of population growth declines in currently underdeveloped economies and they undergo modernizing transformation. First, the relative size of the primary mobile labor reserve will decline as a result of shrinking natural increase. Second, the relative amount of wastage w available for manning expanding sectors will also shrink as agriculture, handicraft industries, and primitive services are drained of underemployed or unemployed personnel. All this, of course, will be a small price to pay for escape from Malthusian traps.

Flexibility in the economy and its labor force can be increased through increase in the flexibility of both labor and industrial structures and equipment. The easier it is for a worker to shift from one type of activity to another, the less he is likely to resist shifting. Furthermore, the easier it is to shunt equipment from one undertaking to another, the less costly in terms of capital and of change-over costs imposed on labor is adjustment to changes flowing from a combination of zero population growth and intersectoral differences in technological progress and elasticity of demand.

7.6. AGE STRUCTURE, EQUITY, AND STABILITY

Social and economic stability are conditioned by whether the opinion prevails that the economy is functioning in a way that makes for increase in equity. In Chapter 4 we noted that age structure bears upon equity, in that in a rapidly growing population young dependents are very numerous, whereas in a stationary population it is old dependents who are very numerous. Those of dependent age are always subject to inequitable treatment, especially in periods of rapid change, because they usually lack not only economic resources but also easily mobilized political power. As we saw in Chapter 4 the three main sources of inequity for persons over 64 (a group that is nearly 50 percent larger in a stationary than in a growing population of given size) are inflation, lack of adequate access to employment, and denial of an equitable share in the fruits of technical progress.

In this section we are concerned with problems of equity for younger persons created by barriers to upward mobility. One barrier has its origin in increasing life expectancy. Today of each 100 males entering the labor force at 20 about 91 or more will be alive at age 60. Seventy years ago only 62 survived to age 60. The second barrier has its origin in the fact that in a stationary population the ratio of older members in the labor force to what we may call preferred positions is greater than it is in a growing population. Suppose that 30 percent of all positions in a society are describable as preferred and relatively more accessible to older persons, especially when experience is somewhat associated with seniority and there are not many new industries to provide preferred posts to enterprising youth (as is the case now in electronics). There is evidence of the pressure of older persons upon the supposedly top 30 percent of positions in society in the statistic that ratio of males in these positions aged 50 to 64 is one-sixth higher in a stationary than in a growing population.

The dissatisfaction these two conditions could create can be reduced if we reduce the gradient of the lifetime-earnings profiles of workers by raising the ratio of earnings in the age period 20 to 30 or 25 to 35 to those in the age period 50 to 64. Such a restructuring of the connection between age and earnings should occasion no difficulty since, as a rule, peak productivity levels are approximated very early in most careers—particularly when (and this is common under modern conditions) productivity patterns are determined by conditions outside labor-force members much more than by continuing experience (as in a much less dynamic society).

Advent of a stationary population would increase the relative scarcity of labor and could therefore, *ceteris paribus,* augment labor's share of the national income (should the ratio of inputs complementary to labor grow rapidly enough to reduce the rate of return on capital and land sufficiently). This would be highly probable in a static economy. It would not result in a dynamic economy, should the substitutability of inputs complementary to and substitutable for labor increase in sufficient measure. Indeed, labor-displacing technological progress could increase substitutability enough to keep the elasticity of demand for capital and the like at levels that serve to keep unchanged or perhaps increase the relative share of net national product imputable to capital and other inputs complementary to labor. The outcome is uncertain, therefore. It depends on the nature and orientation of technological progress and on whether consumer tastes become more or less labor oriented and thus affect the impact of technological progress. Cessation of population growth merely increases the probability that labor's share will rise.

7.7. ZERO POPULATION GROWTH AND THE BEHAVIOR OF SPECIFIC DEMANDS

In Section 7.2 we examined the behavior of aggregate demand in a stationary population. Here we shall touch upon the behavior of demand for specific sets of products and upon the increase of volatility in demand as incomes rise and more of man's time and income become *discretionary* —that is, uncommitted to specific objectives, and easily shiftable from one set of goods and services to another. In an economy such as here described there is little or no correlation between the behavior of demand for most goods and services and the rate of growth of population or its movement in space. The only exceptions are goods, the price and income elasticity of demand for which are very low.

Given so volatile an economy, it is essential that it be flexible and that inputs be highly transformable and/or transferable from one use to another as the composition of the final bill of goods—that is, the composition of the output of goods and services destined for consumers—changes. Such flexibility is conditioned by technological circumstances and by the degree to which trade unions, monopolies, and government policies impede the movement of agents of production in space and between activities.

7.8. ZERO POPULATION GROWTH, POPULATION QUALITY, AND VALUES

It is highly probable that zero population growth will be favorable to population quality. The advent of such a population will mainly be the result of the establishment of a two-child family system about which there will be little variance. Not many women—perhaps 15 to 20 percent —will produce more than two children. As a result a much smaller fraction of the nation's children will be reared in very substandard environments—environments that produce "born losers"—or by parents with inferior genetic equipment. Of far greater importance, the number of children in most families will be in keeping with the capacity of parents to rear well-behaved, technically competent, and socially useful citizens. An agricultural society is suited to the employment of children, but in modern societies few families are capable of rearing more than two children optimally.

The advent of a stationary population would be the product of changes in a nation's structure of values and priorities; it would also contribute importantly to the formation of a new environment of values. The shape this environment might take is not evident. It could, however, have consumption patterns more oriented to space, nature, and the amenities associated with nature. It could also augment the role of the household as producer, given shortening of the work week and work year and the increasingly inadequate and overpriced performance of many sectors of modern economies such as the American.

In what has gone before we have supposed L/P, the ratio of the labor force to the population, to remain unchanged, given a stationary population and hence a stable age structure. If we look at it from the supply side, we might expect L/P to be higher in a stationary than in a growing population. More females would be free of ties connected with child-bearing and rearing and hence able to enter the labor force. With the labor force no longer growing, conditions would be more favorable *ceteris paribus* to lengthening the work lives of both males and females. But whether this would or did happen, it is by no means certain that hours per worker would be reduced enough to offset any increase in L/P. The pattern of values and wants could change in leisure-oriented directions and thus reduce hours worked per member of the labor force and possibly even the L/P ratio.

7.9. POPULATION GROWTH AND EMPLOYMENT

Some people have expressed fear that the advent of a stationary population might be accompanied by an economy wherein employment was less than "full"—say one wherein 5 percent or more of the labor force was unemployed. This fear came to the surface in the 1930s with the Great Depression and the publication of J. M. Keynes's *General Theory of Employment*. Keynes assumed that a high rate of investment was essential, in conjunction with consumption, to keep aggregate demand for output and for labor at the full employment level. Much of the demand for investment—in the neighborhood of half—had its origin in the growth and spread of population. Accordingly, if the rate of population growth were at the zero level, the annual rate of investment would fall far short of the level associated with full employment unless new investment were found to take the place of that formerly originating in the requirements of increments to a nation's population. Such investment would not be easily found since the demand for capital was not very sensitive to reductions in the interest rate. Accordingly, governments would have to pursue fiscal policies suited to increase net expenditures enough to offset the investment shortage that originated in decline in the rate of population growth. In and after the 1940s war- and defense-oriented expenditures combined with population growth to keep aggregate expenditure high. It is possible, however, that should these expenditures cease to grow and the economy remain too inflexible, dearth of demand of the sort Keynes feared could develop. But population growth would be an inferior cure for this even if it were adequate. Moreover, the demand for capital is interest elastic, and many areas of demand, such as collective goods and mass "luxuries," remain little exploited.

7.10. EXPECTATIONS

Every society is shot through with expectations about the future, expectations that vary with group and change in contemporary situation. A society's social and economic stability is conditioned by the degree of compatibility between its expectations and its ability to realize them. These expectations are shaped by the character of a society—by its dynamism and its awareness of trends under way. Current and expected population growth rates are among the determinants of these expectations: expectations, in a stationary population, will be different from those in a growing population.

Decline of the rate of population growth to zero should not reduce compatibility between society's expectations and their realizability, because it does not affect the subjective probabilities that confront individuals, nor does it modify the uncertainty that surrounds the future outcomes of present undertakings and actions. The rate and consequences of population growth change slowly and in ways that are predictable. Population growth is little likely to reduce the impact of risks and uncertainties incident upon an entrepreneur or other decision-maker, because he knows what this growth will be and adjusts his plans accordingly.

A slowing down of population growth tends to increase societal stability, by reducing the relative number who are prone to change and to increase the number who are uncongenial to change for the sake of change. Let us suppose that those in the 15–34 age group are most congenial to change and that those aged 50 to 69 are relatively uncongenial to change, at least to change for the sake of change. Below are the fractions of male populations in these age groups in a stationary population and in populations growing 1.0, 2.0, and 2.5 percent annually given a life expectancy of 71.2 years.

Rate of population growth	0	0.01	0.02	0.025
Percent aged 15-34 years	27.04	30.02	31.87	32.31
Percent aged 50-69 years	22.92	18.02	13.54	11.59
Percent aged 35-49 years	19.76	18.41	16.36	15.18

Evidently a stationary population is less congenial to change than one that is growing. How much the reported differences in age structure actually affect a society's proneness to change is questionable, however; and if it is those in the 35–49 age group that are best situated to generate change, differences in rate of growth become less significant, because this group is relatively larger when a population is stationary than when it is growing. Essentially, since congeniality to change is affected by many circumstances (of which age patterns are but one), generalizations regarding the impact of changes in age structure upon a population's proneness to change are of very limited applicability.

As a population approaches a stationary state its expectations, options, and problems will change. Study will be required to optimize the solution of these problems and permit maximum gains from the emerging options. Such optimization will be facilitated by the slowness with which populations approach a stationary state, together with the greater amount of resources per head available for making the adjustments indicated.

7.11. THE CHOICE

In the end every population is destined to become stationary, as J. S. Mill foresaw, because the environment of every population is supplementable in but minor degree by the environments of other populations. Accordingly, the set of options potentially open to any given population is limited, as is the number of people supportable at any given level of living. Moreover, the length of time a population of given size can be supported depends in part upon the extent of its demands upon the available stock of depletable resources. Presumably, given the choices at hand, many populations may determine to limit their numbers to a maximum far short of some higher fixed number that is sustainable at a lower standard of life. For, while some problems arise or are intensified by the advent of a stationary population, the alternative is less attractive. Moreover, the problems that can arise are manageable.

The distinction between noble and ignoble
wants, between animal and spiritual wants,
rarely makes itself felt by him. . . . As
a result of all this man multiplies himself
more than a wise cooperation of the active and
passive elements in nature would warrant.

J. K. MEHTA, *Rhyme, Rhythm
and Truth in Economics*

Now that we have reviewed most
of the important relations between
demographic variables and socio-economic
variables, it is in order to see their
significance for policy. The term *policy*
implies intervention by the state and its
agencies for the purpose of changing the
rate of population growth, modifying
the distribution of births among elements
of the population, or altering the
distribution of population in space and
among population centers of diverse size.
Such intervention implies, of course,
that when population growth and
distribution in a particular country under
existing conditions are determined entirely
by private decision-makers, the
outcomes are not adequately in keeping
with the welfare of a country's people.

8.1. THE NATURE OF POLICY

Policy may generally be said to
consist in any institutional instrument or
arrangement employed by the state or
polity to realize ends that are unlikely to be

CHAPTER EIGHT

Population Policy

realized in the absence of such instrument or arrangement. Such policy is founded upon one of two justifications. (1) Those who control the apparatus of state seek objectives that are not likely to be achieved if members of the underlying population pursue their individual purposes. (2) While there is general consensus on the content of welfare, it is imperfectly realized because the societal system is shot through with externalities, and so benefits are distributed differently than costs.

Implicit in this is a twofold view of the state. (1) The state is an institution used by those who control its apparatus to serve the purposes of special interests more or less at the expense of the underlying population—sometimes on the ground that "Big Brother knows best" and sometimes with even less justification. Interparty and other political contests are essentially contests for control of the apparatus of state—in "democracies" these contests are between coalitions that are subject to the constraints of the electorate. (2) The role of the state is to guard the integrity of the private sector, to preserve internal and external security, to perform economic and social functions that the state supposedly can do better than private institutions, and to assure a high degree of equity and balance between the costs incident upon individuals and the benefits flowing to them.

The power exercisable by those who man the apparatus of state (the ruling circle, legislature, bureaucracy) is limited in various ways. In small democracies and relatively primitive societies the absence of a strong bureaucratic, military, and police apparatus prevents much exercise of power by the state. In all states the state apparatus is constrained by operative ethical norms, philosophies such as that the individual has absolute "natural rights," and the ability of the population to sabotage distasteful state policies. In "democracies" (as distinguished from absolutist states such as communist states, fascist states, and states on the seventeenth-century Bourbon model) feedback from the electorate holds down the disparity between policy determined at the state level and the concerns of the underlying population.

Demographic policies have always reflected both the degree of a state's absolutism and the concerns of articulate elements in the underlying population. In the past population growth has been encouraged by military and imperial interests in need of manpower, by many living in undersettled lands, by employers in search of "cheap" labor, by ecclesiastical authorities who attached weight to the increase of souls, and by those who feared a country's "depopulation" (for example, France). The policies they enacted were usually not notably successful, except for the immigration-favoring policies of America and present-day Australia. Control of numbers has also had support over the centuries, from proponents of the city-state (Plato, Aristotle), from those who sought to preserve the "quality" or composition of a population, and especially from those since Malthus who were concerned lest population growth affect welfare unfavorably. Today the emphasis is mainly upon population control, though should net reproduction fall below the replacement level (as happened in some countries in the early 1930s) there would probably be support for birth-stimulating policies and complementary "welfare" programs.

8.2. ECONOMIC CONDITIONS AND POPULATION POLICY

Population policy cannot produce welfare so well as it might when an economy is less than optimally flexible. By a flexible economy we mean one that responds quickly to changes in the structure and pattern of demand. Quick response is possible when factors of production, members of the labor force in particular, can shift rapidly from one line of activity to another; then the structure of the available supply of labor can be kept adjusted to the composition of the demand for labor. Capacity for quick response enables an economy to adjust easily to changes in the rate of population growth at national and local levels. Such response implies that interoccupational movement is not prevented by lack of education or the presence of man-made barriers.

As we noted in Chapter 7, from a demographic point of view laborforce mobility, or the capacity to shift from one employment to another, is particularly important. Barriers to mobility have their ultimate origin in specialization. For example, suppose there are but three categories of employment—A, B, and C—and that composition of the demand for labor under ideal conditions requires that 40, 35, and 25 percent, respectively, of the labor force be enrolled in categories A, B, and C. This ideal composition cannot be realized if entry into any category, say A, is controlled as it was under the guild system in and after the Middle Ages and as it is today when a trade union or a professional licensing body denies qualified persons entry into A.

It may be, however, that some members of the labor force are incapable of performing the functions associated with particular employments. For example, 50 percent of the labor force might meet the requirements of category C, but only 25 percent those of A or B. Under these circumstances, the ratio of earnings in C to those in A and B would be very low, and there might not be enough demand for labor in C to absorb the entire number meeting its requirements. If, however, some of those qualified for C could find employment in A or B on a probationary basis and at a temporarily low level of earnings, they might become competent to meet A or B requirements.

Category C may be said to represent persons possessed of very little of the skill required in (say) a modern economy—persons like unskilled blue-collar workers and marginal clerical workers in a highly developed economy. Many persons who answer to this description may have been born, reared, and "educated" in culturally submarginal environments, or their "natural intelligence" may be limited. It might then be difficult to transform enough of these persons into individuals competent to fill vacancies in occupations A and B.

This situation suggests the limitations of fiscal policy as a means of eliminating unemployment. The attainability of "full employment," however defined, is conditioned by the quality of the children brought into the world, the adequacy of the environments in which they grow up, and the degree of compatibility between the price and the productivity of labor. It is desirable, therefore, not only to prevent the birth of genetically inferior children, but also to eliminate "slum" and similar environments, because individuals shaped in these environments find it very difficult to fill employments of the sort found in modern economies.

The argument to this point has been to stress the importance of an economy's flexibility and to note that flexibility is affected by the environments in which children are born and reared. Economic factors also condition the level of fertility and the distribution of population in space. These factors, their effects, and their control will be dealt with below.

The flexibility of economies can be increased not only through appropriate education and prevention of the concentration of economic power in the hands of trade unions, monopolies, and oligopolies, but also through adaptation of technology to the needs of countries, especially those that are less developed and relatively small, as most countries are. Engineering needs to be directed to the development of (1) equipment that requires relatively low capital-labor ratios, and (2) miniaturization of plants so that most or all of the scale economies embedded in large-scale plants can be realized in small-scale plants. With these developments, industrialization and some measure of exportation of manufactured products can progress in underdeveloped countries, along with urbanization and improvement in the distribution of population in space. At present these developments are hindered by the degree to which underdeveloped countries are dependent upon advanced countries for equipment—equipment that has been designed to meet the needs of advanced countries. It may be possible, however, for underdeveloped countries to cooperate in the production of equipment suited to their needs.

8.3. EXCESSIVE FERTILITY

The most fundamental objective of population policy is control of fertility. Fertility is under effective control and at or near the replacement rate in only 20 to 25 percent of the world's population. These countries, most of them economically well developed, are of two sorts: those whose fertility was in the neighborhood of the replacement level in the early 1930s, and those that were transformed by defeat in World War II (Eastern Europe, Japan). Presumably if all unwanted births were averted, fertility would be at the replacement level in Northern America, much of Europe, and parts of the Soviet Union. If this be true, as it appears to be in the United States, then making effective means of birth control available to all elements in the population and emphasizing careful family planning would reduce fertility to the replacement level.

Far more is called for in the countries of the underdeveloped world, where incomes are very low by Western standards, the pressure of numbers upon land and other resources is very great, the net reproduction rate is usually near or above 2.0, and population grows at 1.75 to 2.75 percent per year. The impossibility of the continuation of such growth may be suggested if we project the populations of the world's less-developed regions (LDR) at 2 percent per year. In Table 8-1 we give the populations of these countries as of 1960, together with population densities as of 1960 and 2060. Density is expressed in inhabitants per square kilometer, with acres per person in 2060 in parentheses. In 1960 Japan had 252 people per square kilometer, or about one acre per person, and was already partly dependent on foreign sources for food and raw materials. Given an increase of 2 percent per year in the underdeveloped world, from 2021 million to 15 billion, together with an increase of the population of the developed world to (say) 2 billion, world population density

Table 8-1

Population Density, by World Region, 1960 and 2060

Region	Population (million)	Density, 1960 (km.²)	Density, 2060 (km.²)
LDR low density	494	10	72 (3.43)
LDR moderate density	1480	65	468 (0.53)
LDR high density	47	181	1303 (0.19)
Total	2021	27	194 (1.27)
World	2998	22	126 (1.96)

Source: *United Nations*, World Population Prospects *(1966), p. 27.*

in 2060 would approximate 126 per square kilometer, land per person about 2.0 acres. Arable land per person would be slightly below one-half acre, since only about one-fourth of the world's landed area is potentially arable. If population septuples by 2060, arable land per person would decline to 0.9 acre or below in Africa, to around 0.12 in Asia, and to 1.3 in South America; and if population doubles in Australia, New Zealand, North America, and the Soviet Union, arable land per person in these parts would decline to about 1.5 acres. Neither the world as a whole nor its parts can long support the burden of continuing population growth at present levels, particularly with water shortages imminent in Europe, parts of North and South America, and Asia.

Arguments of the need for very effective measures of population control in the underdeveloped world are reinforced by data relating to income. This world contains about seven-tenths of the world's people, and will account for about five-sixths of all natural increase in the 1970s. Yet in 1961 average income there was only 8 to 9 percent as high as average income in the developed world, and since 1961 the spread between the two has increased, in part because population has grown twice as fast in the underdeveloped world as in the developed world.

8.4. THE MEANS TO FERTILITY CONTROL

The means directly and indirectly conducive to control of fertility are multiple because the economic and social factors that condition fertility are numerous and varied in impact. In every society people of reproductive age are exposed to many conduct-determining stimuli that bear upon fertility. Information flows to them through a variety of channels. Everyone finds himself in a universe of rewards and penalties, some of them conducive to fertility, some of them unfavorable. The potential parent acts in the light of his subjective estimates of the costs and benefits he expects to find associated with childbearing and childrearing in his universe of rewards and penalties. The effectiveness of his response may be conditioned, of course, by the means of fertility control at his disposal and his skill at their use.

In identifying factors that influence utility in varying degree, we shall devote most of our attention to motives that control fertility, given easy availability of relatively inexpensive and effective means to birth regulation. For without easy access to such means, control cannot be sufficiently effective in a modern society with low mortality. In every country and social milieu, therefore, easy access to means of control is absolutely essential to reducing fertility to the replacement level. In some advanced countries fertility may well descend to the replacement level, given such access. In the United States, where one-eighth or more of all births reportedly are unwanted, and the birth expectations of married women born in 1947–1953 suggested that women born in this period might not average over 2.2 births, fertility fell to the replacement level in 1972. Expectations may, of course, change. Prevention of unwanted births may require strengthening of the motivation to control fertility, however, inasmuch as carelessness frequently accompanies sexual relations.

Response to particular motives and variation therein differs from person to person, the same way that response to variation in the prices of goods or services varies. Accordingly, one cannot say that because some individuals fail to respond to limited variation in the strength of a particular stimulus absence of such variation indicates universal insensitivity thereto. One may as well say that because the demand of a particular individual for a particular product is insensitive to a limited change in its price the collective demand for this product is correspondingly insensitive. It is sufficient change in a variety of fertility-affecting stimuli that can produce notable change therein, and not, as a rule, change in one or two isolated stimuli.

Factors affecting fertility are macro-social or micro-social in effect. Under the former are changes in the ideational, ideological, legal, philosophical, and social environments that bear upon most or all individuals rather than on specific individuals in circumscribed situations (which is what micro-social stimuli do). Illustrative of macro-social factors are the regnant doctrine of rights, the nature of the social security system, values, changes in options, flows of information, and so on.

Current opinion about rights and obligations conduces to fertility by neglecting the rights of unborn children and therefore needs to be restructured to make for rational control of fertility. For example, the General Assembly of the United Nations in 1969 and the International Conference on Human Rights in 1968 endorsed the view (expressed already by earlier U.N. bodies) that although sovereign states could formulate and promote population policies, couples had a basic human right to decide freely and responsibly on the number and spacing of their children and the right to adequate education and information about family planning. Neglected in such statements are adverse externalities and, above all, emphasis upon the rights of children to be born with healthy bodies, adequate mental faculties, and in social and physical environments that can develop their potentialities. Only when these rights are taken into account, and parenthood treated as a privilege rather than a right, will well-bornness be widespread, and will families tend to something like optimum size—a size that enables not only adequate material investment but also adequate parental care and supervisory attention to children.

Not many families of over three will be necessary in most countries to replace a population wherein most families include two children, since the replacement level when most women marry will lie between 2.1 and 2.5 children per woman. In other words, parenthood is not denied; what is denied is the alleged right to bring children into environments that can't develop children's potentials. (It is also advisable, of course, that parenthood be denied bearers of extremely defective genes.)

Of the functions of the family (providing economic and other security as well as affection) one that is particularly conducive to fertility and, in instances of sterility, to adoption is parents' dependence on their children for support in old age. But if there are social security systems that assure adequate security in old age, parents will not have the incentive to produce more than two children, if that many. In contrast, parents in underdeveloped countries that are without social security systems and with high infant and child mortalities are bent upon guarding themselves against a shortage of children and thus support. In the event that infant and child mortality prove below average, they may end up with large families. In general, any shift of functions from the family to some metafamily organization (state, lodge, society) will tend to reduce the importance of family and children and thus reduce fertility.

A corollary to the finding that social security reduces parents' dependence on children is the sometime finding that a decrease in infant and child mortality reduces fertility. This finding implies the existence of a target number of living children, depending upon the parents' expectations for their children and upon parental assessment of the probability of survival. Of course when children early become productive, as in the United States in the eighteenth century, their early productiveness removes concern respecting the ability of parents to support them. Under these circumstances support of parents in old age becomes largely a by-product.

Somewhat parallel to the shift of responsibility for support of the aged from children to the state or collectivity is the shift of responsibility for individual security within a multitribe society from tribe to the overall community. If individuals must seek security through the tribe and its position vis-à-vis other tribes, there may be tribal pressure on potential parents to produce more children and thus strengthen a tribe numerically relative to other tribes.

The values that prevail in a country or among segments of a population (say segments held together by beliefs or ideology) exercise an independent influence upon fertility, with other conditions given. Values are not constant, however; they tend to be weakened, strengthened, or otherwise reoriented by change, especially economic change. Indeed, what appear to be values or attitudes may be the result of earlier, favorable experiences that proved the ability of the value in question to yield utility and hence to be worthy of continued acceptance as a guiding principle, after the manner of Sumner's folkways and mores. As conditions change and the value loses utility, it will no longer bear significantly upon fertility.

Changes in the character of a society and in the number of options open to a population may affect fertility. Suppose the options increase. Man's capacity to consume will also increase as his income rises, but only within limits, because capacity to consume is limited by a consumer's time and physical energy. Since the reproduction and rearing of children also consume time and energy, increase in man's options will tend to reduce the relative importance of children and hence diminish fertility. Diminution in options tends to have an opposite effect.

Earlier we mentioned the objective and subjective costs and benefits of children, and that the decision to produce a child, insofar as it is rational, is based on comparison of the subjective, estimated costs with the subjective, estimated benefits. Improvement in the flow of information should bring these subjective estimates into greater compatibility with objective conditions and thus increase or decrease fertility, depending upon whether subjective costs have been overestimated or underestimated.

Fertility is affected also by a society's tax and subsidy systems, since these systems affect the objective costs of children incident upon parents and hence their assessment of subjective costs. A family allowance system stimulates fertility, at least in the short run, and also in the long run unless it operates to increase the subjective standard of life of the children more than enough to counterbalance the stimulus given fertility when these children reach reproductive age. Fundamentally at issue in the somewhat longer run, therefore, is whether the allowance system eventually tilts the subjective cost-benefit ratio against fertility. Presumably an allowance system continues on balance to stimulate fertility, as does a tax system or any other system of impositions or grants that favors parents relative to nonparents and thus shifts some potential parents at the margin toward parenthood.

Turning to the micro or family level of the costs and benefits of children, especially to the estimates of potential parents, we may say that whatever is believed to elevate the cost relative to the benefit at the margin is likely to make fertility lower than it would otherwise be, and conversely. Such an outcome may result from a perceived change in costs and benefits in the absence of externalities, or from an increase or decrease in the degree to which costs or benefits are shunted to people other than the parents responsible for these costs and benefits.

As I have suggested, increase (or decrease) in the availability of opportunities to work, save, recreate, or secure relatively attractive housing, material objects, or any other object that absorbs time, energy, and purchasing power that might otherwise have been devoted to reproducing and rearing children will tend to reduce (or increase) fertility. Increase (decrease) in the prices of goods and services that affect the cost of bearing and rearing children vis-à-vis the costs of competing goods and services will tend to diminish (increase) fertility. Similarly, increase in the time horizon governing the decision process that relates to the production and rearing of another child will probably diminish fertility if it places greater emphasis upon the prospective course of family income and outlay and thus intensifies uncertainty and consciousness of the usually upward trend of costs incident on parents.

Perception of the costs and perhaps assessment of benefits from the bearing and rearing of children may be sharpened if awareness of these costs and benefits can be developed early. This can be accomplished by requiring parents to initiate a combination insurance and savings plan at the time of a child's birth that assures the child of the subsequent availability of its educational, medical, and other wants normally incident upon the family purse. Such early awareness is important because, as we noted earlier, the cost per child-year rises significantly as the child ages, faster usually than parental income.

If the object of policy is to reduce fertility, two courses of action are indicated, each of which acts directly or indirectly on the stimuli incident upon man. First, the macro-social environment needs to be oriented more against fertility. This will tilt the universe of penalties and rewards somewhat against fertility, but changes at the micro-level and requisite knowledge and easy access to effective means of fertility regulation are also essential. Some fertility-affecting functions hitherto connected with the family need to be shunted to other organizations, and the marginal ratio of anticipated costs of childbearing and childrearing to anticipated benefits must be increased. Among the means to accomplishing this increase is making all costs of childbearing and childrearing incident upon responsible parents. Of course should such internalization of costs reduce fertility unduly (an outcome at all likely only in some developed countries) some cost relief can be introduced, or externalized benefits can be restored to parents.

In recent years, largely under the stimulus of Stephen Enke's proposals, small financial rewards are bestowed upon potential parents for abstaining from parenthood, or from having more than a permitted number of children. The return to the country on such investment is very great—ten or more times the cost—since the cost of children is many times the cost of sterilizing a potential parent or of inducing him or her to employ some effective means of birth control. In the event that the method of control is impermanent (pill, I.U.D.) it becomes necessary not only to repeat payments but in the end to construct institutional pressures upon the potential parents to restrict family size to the sought level.

The forces that operate upon fertility fall into three categories: (1) those internalized in many members of a society (habits, values), (2) those imbedded in particular socio-economic or societal systems, and (3) those of a more transitory character (payments for use of contraceptives—such as the pill—that are effective for short periods only). It is essential, therefore, that transitory means (3) be supported by (1) or (2).

Whether the disposition to control births will spread at an increasing rate, as suggested by a logistic theory of diffusion, is not clear. The incremental rate of diffusion should increase, at least until the fraction of the population not practicing birth control has fallen to half. In some underdeveloped countries a bandwagon movement could get under way, provided that nonrecourse to birth control is associated with a belief on the part of each household head that his recourse to birth control would be strongly disapproved by those with whom he is in contact—because then, when this belief is found to be without basis, birth control might spread rapidly, perhaps in keeping with the pattern underlying logistic models. When births are subject to effective control the birth rate can become volatile, rising when it becomes fashionable to have children early and at short intervals, declining when problems associated with the upsurge in natality become apparent.

It is unlikely that effective steps to control fertility will be taken in developing countries in the near future. There is too little understanding of the costs of continuing population growth, a disinclination to accept adequate technological help from advanced countries, and, in many countries, an insufficiently strong civil service to carry out effective family planning programs. All this is not surprising, in view of the ineffectiveness and ambivalence of population programs in advanced countries. It is possible, of course, that intensifying population pressure will spur action, particularly if it is realized that each delay of a decade adds many millions to a nation's numbers.

8.5. POPULATION DISTRIBUTION

Because population growth in regions and cities is cumulative—and migrants may remain attracted to urban and regional concentrations that already have passed critical sizes—population distribution is likely to become suboptimal. For example Central Sweden is drawing population out of North Sweden and Finland, while Scotland, Wales, Ireland, and Brittany are losing people to more prosperous regions. Such movements are likely to originate in conditions of low wages and unemployment, conditions that are often structural in character and the result of earlier inflexibility. At issue is not movement of population as such—such movements being essential to economic development and the optimization of population distribution—but concentration in excess of the level compatible with maximization of welfare and average income. Optimum distribution in space is not likely to be realized in the absence of governmental intervention; there are too many externalities and too little information available to most individuals.

Most underdeveloped countries contain relatively small urban components, and so they still have options respecting population distribution that advanced lands no longer have. For example in 1960 only one-fifth of the population of underdeveloped countries was urban, compared with 58 percent in Europe. Accordingly, many underdeveloped countries can still plan the distribution of their population, but they may be handicapped by a high rate of natural increase and by the consequent persistence of the rural character of the population. If a population that is four-fifths rural grows 2 percent per year, and the urban growth rate is 3 percent, about a century and a half must pass before the rural population is reduced in size.

The imminence of water shortages in various parts of the world will shape the future distribution of the world's population, according to C. A. Doxiadis. By around 2050, it has been estimated, urban dwellers, then about nine-tenths of the world's population, will occupy about 5 percent of the earth's surface, along seashores, river banks, and around lakes, at an average density of perhaps 12 per acre. Meanwhile the world's agricultural population will occupy 45 percent of the world's land. The remaining half of the earth's surface—forests, deserts, mountains, and plains—would function as a watershed.

Proposals and estimates of this sort do not seem practical on political, economic, or technological grounds, but they do suggest the importance of some locational determinants and their impact upon population distribution. They neglect the role of the forces that can influence the location of employment opportunities (see Chapter 2). We have touched earlier upon the adverse effects of imbalance between private costs and private benefits associated with the growth of population concentrations, but we need to consider them again. Their importance derives in part from the fact that private net advantage tends to differ most from the total cost-benefit relation at the fringes of population concentrations. It is here that problems lie, and that there is a basis for public control or ownership of the land surrounding cities, because often, if not always, private speculation in land prevents maximization of the social welfare function of cities and other population concentrations.

Since political constraints on the size of a city or state may become operative and sources of increasing cost before economic constraints, maximizing political welfare may call for greater dispersal of population then do economic circumstances alone. Careful attention needs to be given, therefore, to both political and noneconomic determinants of welfare, for realization of an overall population optimum is likely to call for a smaller national population or city-size than do economic circumstances alone.

All this dissipation must in some way be balanced if the regime is to continue.

The extinction of a species seems to follow, not infrequently, close upon its period of greatest development.

A. J. Lotka

Up to this point I have dealt with important aspects of the population question from both national and world points of view. In this chapter, essentially a postscript, I focus upon some of the major issues of population policy.

9.1. GROUNDS FOR CONTROL OF POPULATION GROWTH

There are six basic grounds for the control of numbers. They can be examined in both a world and a national context.

1. The physical environment at the world and at national levels is finite, hence of finite load-bearing capacity. This environment is composed of a very large number of ecosystems. Though local in situation, these ecosystems are actually or potentially interrelated, in that disruption of one is likely to affect others. Man may be said to live in a worldly web of life that is shot through with pressure thresholds, trespass of which can create disturbances that can spread out from the area of origin. Forces that make for stability are not always powerful enough to offset local pressures for instability. We have divers

CHAPTER NINE

The Road Ahead: Issues

evidence of this in the detritus of organic life that was formerly dominant and in changes evident in man's physical environment. Moreover, the rate of change is increasing. Since 1600 A.D., according to careful studies, at least 120 major species of birds and mammals have become extinct, and another 100 are destined to disappear in the next 20 to 50 years. These disappearances are mainly imputable to pressure upon the species beyond their capacity to accommodate, and most of that pressure originated in the growth of man's numbers and activities.

Pressure on the biosphere and environment man lives in is increasing at a high if not accelerating rate. In 1960 the world's population (3 billion) was about 12 to 15 times as large as at the start of the Christian era, and average consumption must have been 10 to 15 times as high. Accordingly, man's total pressure upon his finite habitat in 1960 was something like 120 to 225 times as great as at the start of the Christian era. Should world population increase no more than 100 percent by the year 2000, and average consumption rise 1.5 percent per year, pressure will be something like 3.6 times what it was in 1960. Moreover, if the combined impact of growth of population and average consumption increases 2 percent per year in the twenty-first century, it will be 7.2 times as great in 2100 as in 2000, 26 times as great as in 1960, and perhaps 500 or more times as great as in the days of Augustus Caesar. These estimates are hypothetical, but they do indicate the order of magnitude of the growth of man's pressure upon his habitat.

Such crude measures may not, however, bring out adequately the growth of this pressure. Some parts of man's environment are more significant, given his technology and style of life, than are others. These parts may feel the pressure in greater degree, therefore, than does the environment as a whole, particularly if the forces of depletion and pollution cannot be countervailed by technological improvements and the discovery or development of substitutes for the parts in question.

This increase in pressure has its origin in man's growth in number and average consumption. In some countries (India, China, Indonesia) it is associated mainly with growth in population; in others with growth in average income (United States); and in still others (Japan, parts of Western Europe) with growth of both. Each source weighs upon selected components of man's physical and organic environment, and while this pressure is experienced immediately in national or regional spheres, it is not confined thereto, because international commerce propagates this pressure from areas where it is initially felt, thus equalizing the distribution of its impact and also making it much greater than it otherwise would be. For example, if country X is a heavy importer of particular raw materials, it uses more of these than it would if they were not to be had in foreign markets. Such importation does not significantly affect consumption elsewhere in the short run, since the supply price of the raw materials is not likely to be augmented greatly in the short run—or if it is augmented it does not greatly increase the final cost of many of the products the raw materials are used for. In the longer run, however, the cumulative impact of productive processes that use inputs becomes an effective barrier to growth when the sources of these inputs are fixed in amount or subject to depletion.

Internationally diffused pressure grows and spreads most rapidly when there are few or no political or social barriers to its diffusion. Within a country the principle of private property, together with functionally equivalent principles, tends to restrict rates of resource use according to the productivity of the country's resources. But when resources lie outside the political control of any country, exploitation is carried out in disregard of the future. Even potentially self-sustaining resources are exploited at rates that ensure their eventual destruction. Cases in point are various kinds of edible or otherwise utilizable ocean fish that are unprotected by the property principle and little protected by so-called treaty provisions. Consequently, these fish are being taken at rates far in excess of their replenishing capacity. As a result utilizable species will disappear and the composition of the biomass of the sea will become less and less useful to man.

International diffusion of pollutants operates in a somewhat parallel fashion. It is not controlled effectively by enforceable international agreements, and as a consequence the environments of countries can be rendered less useful by pollutants originating in other countries. Control of population, or at least of the effects of its increase, is a matter of international concern, as the 1972 International Conference on Issues of Environmental Control recognized.

2. The foregoing relates mainly to the impact of the replacement of smaller populations with smaller Gross National Products by those that are larger and consume at higher average rates. The impact of the population-growth process as such is at least as significant, because it entails absorption of goods and services that might otherwise be devoted to the increase of average output and welfare. To illustrate, suppose that a nation's population grows 2 percent annually, and that this growth absorbs about one-tenth of the nation's productive power. Since marginal investment yields 10 percent, if this absorbed increment of productive power were diverted from investment in population growth to investment in increasing the per capita rate of growth y', it might raise the latter from (say) 0.01 to 0.02. Over a century the 0.02 rate would increase average income by 7.24 times, compared with 2.7 times for the 0.01

rate. Increase in average income and consumption may of course increase pressure on man's biosphere nearly as much as a corresponding increase in population.

3. The pressure of man *against* man in finite space is also increasing rapidly. As we noted earlier, if every person were equally likely to be thrown in contact with every other person in a community, theoretically his exposure to contact would increase roughly as n^2, where n designates a community's population. Of course, because of social and physical barriers that separate every individual from many other individuals, exposure of a given individual to contact with all others does not increase so rapidly. It does increase, however, as numbers grow and as increase in a person's geographical and social mobility enables him to surmount various barriers. A limited amount of increase in personal contact is welcomed by individuals and essential to increase in their productivity, but some forms of contact affect man's welfare adversely. Indeed, as pressure of man upon man increases, increase in antisocial behavior tends to follow, with the result that more collective control of individual behavior becomes necessary. Accordingly, mere increase in interhuman pressure may become a stimulus both to limit numbers and to disperse population in space.

4. Inequality in the international distribution of income is greater today than it was 100 to 150 years ago. The disparity has not yet begun to decrease, and it could increase. Many factors account for this, some of them accentuated by the relatively high rates of population growth that came in this century as a consequence of introducing death control into the economically underdeveloped world. With no accompanying birth control, the rate of natural increase rose from under one percent to 2 to 3 percent and higher—to levels much above those of Japan and Europe after economic development got under way, or even of the United States in and after the late nineteenth century. Income inequality cannot be eliminated, but it probably can be reduced, though not unless numbers are brought under control in the very near future.

Combine these grounds for control with the prediction that world food requirements will match the world's food-producing capacity in a few decades, and one can see the importance of reducing the Net Reproduction Rate to the replacement level soon. Even if this were to be accomplished early in the next century, world population would still be around 7 to 8 billion, double the current world population. Yet the world rate of growth remains in the neighborhood of 2 percent.

5. Disparity tends to emerge between the costs of population growth and its benefits (if any). (This is much less characteristic of simple agricultural economies than of modern industrial economies which tend

to be increasingly characterized by such disparity.) Let C be costs associated with fertility (as in Chapter 5), and B the benefits associated with C. Costs are divisible into C_1, those incident upon the individual whose behavior occasions C, and C_e, those incident on others. We can divide B similarly, into B_i, the benefits flowing to the agent responsible for C, and B_e, those flowing to others. Fertility is stimulated when B_1 is greater than C_1, even though C is greater than B, and it is discouraged when C_e is greater than B_e even though B is greater than C. When the distribution of costs begins to differ notably from that of benefits, collective intervention becomes necessary.

6. We can say that most people have a collective or social welfare function—a kind of consensus to which most persons subscribe or submit. One of the elements of this function is the number of a country's inhabitants, since it affects the level of average income and perhaps other elements as well. Another is the rate of population growth, since it conditions the growth rate of average income, educational opportunity, and perhaps other elements. A country's people should settle upon how many people and what rate of natural increase it wants; then, if neither the number nor the growth rate is automatically realized, there is ground for collective intervention.

9.2. GROUNDS FOR CONTROLLING POPULATION DISTRIBUTION

The welfare of populations—of the world and of particular countries—depends upon how population is distributed in space and among urban communities. At the world level, however, there is little likelihood of change in distribution; very few countries welcome immigrants in large numbers, and most of those that do admit immigrants stipulate occupational and other qualifications. The great age of essentially unregulated international migration that flourished after the close of the Napoleonic wars ended with the outbreak of World War I, and now individual sovereign countries are inclined to admit immigrants only if their admission is deemed advantageous (political refugees are the main exception to this).

Heavily populated countries must seek partial relief in the form of international trade, which within limits is now a substitute for international migration. A country that is heavily peopled and short of natural resources can engage in the production of goods and services of which labor is a relatively high proportion, though realization of this comparative advantage requires access to markets in relatively less densely populated countries. In general, therefore, population pressure can be somewhat relieved through freedom of international trade.

Within countries, however, one may find great potential for control of distribution. When overall population density is low, the per capita use of land can generally be relatively high, whereas high density necessitates greater efforts to economize the use of land surface. The response of the price structure to the degree of land scarcity will affect the distribution of population, though seldom adequately, because, as we have already explained, population distribution depends mainly upon distribution of employment opportunities, and this distribution is affected by determinants of industrial location, the evolution of transport, chance, and diverse other circumstances. These stimuli rarely produce a population distribution wholly compatible with the social welfare index described in (6) in Section 9.1. Because of externalities and spillover effects, a disparity between the distribution of costs and benefits may make for suboptimum distribution of numbers in space unless there is intervention by the state along lines suggested in (5) in Section 9.1.

9.3. PROSPECTS FOR CONTROL

Control of numbers or of population distribution in space will not come about automatically, because the costs and benefits associated with population growth are so distributed that those responsible for births do not have to bear most of the costs. Even if these costs were incident upon the parents, it would not follow that fertility would decline to near the replacement level, because many persons are unable or unwilling to control fertility effectively. In the United States, for example, many unwanted births occur even though contraceptive means are generally accessible. Requisite besides accessibility to these means is the will and the competence to use these means effectively.

It is clear that the state must intervene if fertility is to be brought under effective control. Many governments have expressed concern at population growth and have adopted family-planning policies, but such policies have not, as a rule, accomplished much. Toothless policies are seldom effective.

A condition that favors effective control of fertility is the increase in the power of the modern state. The technological equipment at its command and the skills of its bureaucracy give it greater power than ever before. Accordingly, even though public bureaucratic organizations tend to be less effective than comparable organizations in the private sector, the state can exercise a great deal of influence in realizing particular ends— among them those bearing upon questions of population. The ends to be sought and the effectiveness of that quest depend significantly upon the elements in society that control the apparatus of state. During the past century control of this apparatus has passed increasingly, not to the masses or to the common man as such, but to organizations representing the common man, organizations like trade-unions and some political parties. As a result the concerns that dominated governmental policy in the eighteenth and early nineteenth centuries have largely been displaced by those with appeal to the common man. Hence questions of population policy will depend heavily upon the appeal that policy proposals have to the common man and to his spokesmen. And since a zero or very low rate of population growth should conduce to increase in the equity of income distribution, the common man should support such a very low rate of population growth. (A partial exception to this may occur in states wherein power is highly centralized, wherein the state is less the agent than the master of the underlying population. But even in states so constituted those in control may find their power to regulate population growth very limited if policy runs counter to the wants of the underlying population.)

In a sense population policy reflects the vision a society has of its future and the role of population growth in this vision. This vision in turn reflects three sets of forces: those constituting the ruling ideological orientation, those embedded in the flow of solid information, and those underlying governance of the economy, the apparatus of state, and the intergroup and interclass distribution of political and economic power. Of ideological orientations we shall only say here that they condition the ends sought in a society and affect response to the flow of solid information, tending to distort its interpretation and use. The degree to which ideological considerations can affect the use of information is, of course, limited in modern societies in that the stock of relevant information usually is great and cumulating and quite well diffused. Accordingly, while ideology may affect sought ends significantly, it cannot greatly affect the manner in which ends are sought. This is evident in the degree to which economies that are industrialized or merely undergoing industrialization resemble one another. Views and aspirations of the underlying population will, however, contribute notably to the dominant vision of the future and of the role of population, particularly if political power is widely distributed.

Whether population growth will be brought under effective control turns on whether correct assessment is made of the significance of continued population growth. Unfortunately such assessment might tend to be swamped by the minutiae of economic and demographic planning and by neglect of effective stimuli to control fertility. Ad hoc rewards and penalties can contribute to this end, especially in the short run. In the longer run, however, given widespread access to contraceptive means, the pressures on individuals and families must be institutionalized in an orderly fashion. If these pressures are adequate, they will make for fertility patterns that are compatible with maintenance of a stationary population, or for a small rate of increase in countries with populations of suboptimum size.

A question with two implications must be faced by governments. Heretofore it has been generally accepted that individuals have a "natural right" to procreate within the framework of marriage or functionally equivalent institutions. Such right is often proclaimed by cultists and others who favor large populations for ulterior reasons. Exercise of such a so-called right needs to be subordinated to two overriding conditions. First, births in excess of an average number compatible with maintenance of a stationary population, or with a very low and approved rate of growth, cannot be allowed. Second, the reproduction and rearing of children are too important to be turned over to persons who cannot provide a satisfactory environment for children and equip them with an adequate genetic structure. Unless the so-called right to reproduce is subject to these two constraints it is not very likely that net reproduction can be kept at or near the replacement level and childrearing confined to satisfactory environments.

9.4. METHODS OF CONTROL

Methods of controlling population growth or distribution are of three interrelated forms. (1) Efforts may be made to internalize in individuals, especially in the young, a set of moral or ethical objectives or rules that channel man's behavior in keeping with a society's welfare objectives, functioning in respect of man's behavior much as, Lotka suggests, logic functions in respect of thought. (2) The rewards and penalties to which an individual is subject may be modified, if necessary, to render desirable population objectives more attractive and undesirable population movements less attractive. This may be done by introducing taxes and subsidies into the price structure, or by imposing legal penalties upon those who behave otherwise than in the manner sought.

Methods (1) and (2) stress man's motives and stimulate him to pursue desired demographic courses. The methods under (3) are designed to make it easier for man to pursue these courses and hence to increase the probability that stimuli under (1) and (2) will prove adequate. Improvements in methods of contraception or in man's capacity to locate his activities freely in space are illustrative of (3). Methods under (3) thus are technological in nature, consisting in new instruments or in changes in man's physical environment. These methods depend for success upon man's realization that they are not substitutes for (1) and (2) but complements to the latter and intended to make stimuli under (1) and (2) adequate by reducing the various costs of desired behavior.

Technological improvements may ease the task of avoiding externalities and spillover effects and of internalizing the costs and benefits of demographic behavior and making both wholly incident upon the parties responsible. Inquiry into the limitations of technology serves to isolate areas of behavior in which recourse to ethics or price variation or both is necessary. Such inquiry is especially important in respect of population policy, since improvements in technology can facilitate but cannot motivate fertility control.

Technology can contribute greatly also to population decentralization. It can do this principally by miniaturizing optimum plant size and hence reducing scale economies and the degree that economic activities need to be concentrated to yield advantages associated with agglomeration of activities. Miniaturization need not entail much if any decrease in the capital-labor ratio, which would run somewhat counter to the tendency for the substitution of capital for labor to reduce the size of the work force associated with a given plant.

There are limits to what technology can accomplish, of course. Illustrative are limits to its capacity for overcoming the shrinkage in man's utilizable environment. Exploitation of this environment has been intensified by the growth of man's numbers and even more by increase in his average consumption and his consequent need to overcome increasing drafts upon materials, energy, and nutrients. Indeed, growth in numbers has increased each of what S. Brubaker describes as man's five principal environmental hazards: global climate, radioactivity, pesticides, agricultural wastes, and soil erosion. Technological change may help to cushion the incidence of these hazards, and decentralization of population may reduce the overall intensity of the incidence of pollutants, but it cannot stop their growth. Effective control of numbers through methods (1) and (2) is the only final answer.

9.5. DEMAND AND EMPLOYMENT

Two kinds of unemployment problems are associated with rates of population growth. (1) In underdeveloped economies unemployment tends to persist because productive agents that are complementary to labor, especially capital, increase less rapidly than the labor force. This is because there is a limit to the degree to which labor can be substituted for other agents and the ratio of these agents to labor reduced. The stock of these agents must therefore be increased rapidly enough to combine with a rapidly growing labor force. If this is not done and the labor force grows more rapidly than these agents, unemployment increases and average consumption falls.

(2) Unemployment may also rise, Keynesian models suggest, if investment and other offsets to savings do not grow so fast as savings at the full-employment level of activity. Insofar as this argument is valid the state may need to intervene with public expenditure upon investment as well as consumption of goods and services and thereby bring total expenditure to the level commensurate with the rate and growth of savings at the full-employment level.

Unemployment may reflect other demographic changes. It may rise if the composition of output is not kept adjusted to changes in the composition of demand associated with decline in the rate of population growth. It may rise if the rate of population growth is uneven and the economy is not adjusted to this unevenness. Finally, it may rise if the economy is not adjusted to accommodate a much larger number of job-seekers 65 and older.

None of the problems associated with slow or zero population growth will become serious so long as the economy is flexible and man-made barriers to labor mobility are suppressed.

9.6. POLITICAL OUTLOOK

Prognosis for the demographic future of the Spaceship Earth is anything but sanguine. The will to halt population growth is weak in most regions, and the means to control fertility are not well distributed. Presumably the situation in most countries will become worse until political power passes into the hands of those with the will to bring numbers to a halt. The longer such action is delayed, the less correctable the situation will be, and the fewer the options.

A dynamic theory...defines Progress as the development and economy of forces [and] force as anything that does or helps to do work. ... Man's function as a force of nature was to assimilate other forces as he assimilated food.

HENRY ADAMS, *The Education of Henry Adams*

In the preceding chapter we examined grounds for population policy, especially policy relating to population control. In this chapter we shall inquire into the conditions that underlie international inequality in average income, and the relation between these conditions and the size and rate of growth of national populations. Our emphasis is upon the sources of "modernization"—the set of processes closely associated with growth of income and improvement in man's material welfare. We shall identify these sources, then relate them to demographic factors, especially those of potential importance to underdeveloped countries. Since the present world population pattern is the product of the uneven forces of demographic evolution we shall take some note of the historical genesis of the current state of affairs. Not only will such inquiry illuminate the pattern of growth in the past; it will also reveal differences between the English and the Japanese experiences, and how these experiences

CHAPTER TEN   might apply to less modernized countries.

Population and Modernization

10.1. INTRODUCTION

Countries obviously differ widely in degrees of modernization, but there is less agreement regarding how modernization is to be measured and interpreted.

Existing data (see Section 10.3 below) permit classification of countries on the basis of Gross National Product (GNP) per head and GNP rate of growth. Given these averages and changes, one can roughly determine the relative situation of countries and the degree to which these situations are changing. Since average income is highly correlated with, and is a component of, GNP per head, data on the movement of GNP indicate how average income is moving. Moreover, since average income is a very good indicator of the options open to a country and its people, it may serve as a satisfactory indicator of the objective standard of life realizable.

Worth recalling at this point, however, are Alexander Pope's lines about happiness:

> 'Tis nowhere to be found, or everywhere;
> 'Tis never to be bought, but always free.

"Welfare" or "happiness" does not correlate highly with average income or the objective standard of living. Some conditions conducive to "happiness"—health, access to goods and services—are positively associated with level of income, but in limited measure. Moreover, although excessive consumption may be considered harmful, an individual can vary his use of income in keeping with his tastes and health. In general, however, "happiness" is subjective and hence influenced by a variety of conditions many of which are not closely associated with income and quite changeable. We are not to infer, therefore, that free men today are happier than free men in George Washington's time, or that modernization necessarily increases man's happiness.

Because several indicators of modernization are highly correlated with Gross National Product per capita, we can use this indicator to divide the countries of the world into underdeveloped and developed. In 1965 about 32 percent of the world's population lived in developed regions—Europe, USSR, Northern America, Japan, temperate South America, Australia, and New Zealand, but it is predicted that by 2000 this percentage will fall to about 25. Of the population in underdeveloped countries in 1965, about 57 percent were in China, India, and Indonesia, and another 5 percent in what was then Pakistan. The underdeveloped world's population thus is concentrated in and near mainland Asia.

The fraction of a country's labor force that is engaged in agriculture is fairly indicative of its degree of modernization. For, since per capita consumption of agricultural produce usually grows slower than either income per head or output per agriculturalist, the number of agriculturalists required to supply a country's needs increases less rapidly than its labor force and may finally decline, as happened in Western Europe. Hence the relative size of a country's rural population tends to decline as average income rises, for a rural population consists mainly of agricultural population and persons engaged in servicing this population. Between 1920 and 1960 the rural fraction of the world's population decreased from 0.61 to 0.40 in developed regions and from 0.92 to 0.80 in less developed regions; by 2000 the corresponding percentages are expected to approximate 0.19 and 0.59.

10.2. DEMOGRAPHIC FACTORS AND MODERNIZATION

Modernization, from a world point of view, amounts to a process designed to reduce international heterogeneity and increase international homogeneity, and thus reverse a process operative since (say) the late Middle Ages that pulled some communities away from others. Modernization restores power to forces of convergence and substitutes them for the forces of international divergence that have been ascendant for some centuries. This substitution process is conditioned by international differences in fertility. The rapid reduction of fertility and an increase in the capacity of less advanced lands to accept and adapt the ways of thought and action that have made the now advanced lands and their people modern are essential to modernization.

Modernization consists of a variety of changes describable as changes in the "content" of the mind. These changes constitute the "cause" rather than the "product" of changes, both in the manner that society and economy are organized and in the apparatus that man uses to exploit his physical and cultural environment. These changes are reflected in the values and purposes that animate individual and collective behavior. The most conspicuous indicator of modernization is increase in the average output of goods and services. First we shall identify the immediate causes of this increase, and later the less immediate causes. Modernization being a process, some determinants immediately generate income or modernization, others generate change in the immediate determinants This process involves interaction among the determinants and between the changes in average income and population; modification of some of these factors is likely to modify others. It is difficult to estimate with precision the impact of demographic factors upon the determinants of modernization and income growth, or the contribution of each of the immediate determinants of increase to output. It is even more difficult to estimate the contribution of less immediate determinants. The estimates of E. F. Denison and others relate to advanced countries, and give little attention to population problems.

The immediate determinants of increase in output per capita can be divided into those that improve the quality of a population and its labor force and those that increase the amount of productive equipment and other utilizable environment per capita as well as improve the way industry is organized and production agents are combined. When these determinants are classified in greater detail, it is easier to indicate the degree the growth rate of a country's population or its size affects them. Here are twelve of these direct determinants.

1. *The ratio of persons of working age to the population.* As we saw earlier, this ratio is at or near the maximum when a population is growing very slowly or not at all.

2. *The ratio of employed labor force to the population of working age.* A low rate of natural increase is favorable to this ratio, because a low level of fertility enables more women to enter the labor force. The state of a population's health conditions how many of its members desire to enter or remain in the labor force and how regularly those in the labor force are able to perform their duties. Employment is facilitated by a low and *nonfluctuating* rate of natural increase, because then physical and personal capital that is essential to the maintenance of health and employment can be formed at a relatively high and constant rate since the relative number of new entrants into the labor force does not fluctuate markedly.

3. *The quality of the labor force.* This depends mainly upon education and experience. Investment in education is in turn favored by a low rate of natural increase and the age composition associated therewith. Quality is also favored by the state of a population's health, since levels of a labor force's activity are positively correlated with health.

4. *Growth per capita in the size and the rate of use of information that bears upon the output of goods and services.* Growth of this stock depends mainly upon the investment of manpower and equipment in science, but the degree of use depends upon investment in engineering skill adapted to early and full economic exploitation of old and new scientific knowledge of both foreign and domestic origin. Among the results attendant upon a high degree of use is increase in man's incentive and capacity to make further additions to the stock of productive knowledge.

5. *Education and related facilities per capita.* This determinant is

closely related to (3) and (4). Its role is threefold: assimilation of the young into society, distribution of information and capacity for its analysis, and generation of new information and analytical powers. When the rate of natural increase is unduly high, not enough resources and trained manpower can be spared to the educational sector to permit effective fulfillment of the threefold educational role. As a result, the ratio of high-level professional manpower to the labor force remains below the level essential to full modernization, and there are too few responsible and competent persons to exploit a country's potential.

6. *The entrepreneurial skill commonly associated with the business community.* This contributes to the effectiveness with which productive information is used and inputs are allocated to uses in keeping with the wants and demands of a nation's population. A major advantage of a free-enterprise economy over a collective one is that in the former profit-seeking entrepreneurs are forced to search out opportunities for consumer service and to act quickly to supply them, whereas in a collective economy *on the contrary,* both capacity and disposition to meet the wants of the population are encumbered and hampered in many respects. Demographic factors, with the partial exception of how population is distributed in space, have little influence upon the extent and skill of enterprise; for *ceteris paribus* these are associated predominantly with the politico-economic organization of a society.

7. *Physical equipment per worker and per capita.* This ratio tends to be highest *ceteris paribus* when a population is close to optimum size and the rate of population growth is low. This enables a relatively high rate of capital information, which can conduce to a relatively high rate of increase in *reproducible* assets per head; and *pressure* upon *depletable* (minerals) as well as fixed-stock (land) components of man's physical environment increases less rapidly than when the rate of natural increase is high.

8. *Economies of scale.* These make for increase in output per unit of input; they are associated with both size of economy and size of markets served by firms and hence are conditioned, within limits, by the size of a country's population, average income, and population distribution in space. These economies are subject to reduction in importance through technological changes conducive to reduction in plant size and in costs of transport and communication. As we shall see, most underdeveloped countries are too small to maximize economies of scale, so they must achieve these economies through international trade. These economies can be realized in a very few countries, like Canada and Australia, through increase in size of domestic population.

9. *Distribution of population in space.* An underdeveloped country's

population may be both too dispersed and too concentrated in space; so may that of an advanced country. This is mainly the result of non-demographic conditions, but it can be accentuated by regional differences in fertility and natural increase. Correction consists in appropriate redistribution of population and natural increase together with a complementary distribution of new capital and other agents of production. Redistribution can proceed more easily when much of society's savings are not being absorbed by a high rate of population growth; in particular, urbanization can proceed most effectively when the rural and the overall rates of natural increase are low and capital is available to employ rural residents in cities and to increase output per agriculturalist.

10. *International exchange.* As a rule increase in international trade serves, within limits, to increase the aggregate value of a country's current flow of inputs and output. International exchange reduces population pressure in a relatively overpopulated country by augmenting aggregate demand for the services of its labor force. Continuing population growth may, however, increase the volume of its exports in relation to the world market and thereby reduce the terms on which these exports can be sold abroad.

11. *Flexibility of economy.* It is desirable that the agents of production be free to move from areas or occupations in which they are relatively numerous and hence can command only relatively low prices to areas or occupations in which they are relatively scarce and hence can command relatively high prices. Even an optimum interoccupational and interindustrial balance would prove transitory in a dynamic economy. For innovations, being unevenly incident by industry and occupation, increase the output of particular goods and services at very different rates; moreover, the elasticity of demand for goods and services varies greatly, with the result that some markets are much more susceptible of profitable extension than others. Flexibility is governed by the ways that economic power and information are distributed. The burden of maintaining flexibility tends to increase, however, when the rate of natural increase varies greatly by region and occupational category of parents, for then more agents of production must move. At the same time, as I explained earlier, when the rate of increase of the labor force is very low, maintenance of optimum interoccupational balance can prove more difficult than when the rate is somewhat higher. This difficulty is easily overcome, however, if information on employment needs is effectively mobilized and utilized to give appropriate direction to persons newly entering the labor force or interested in changing employment.

12. *State of expectation.* Hope is essential if men are to face the future as laden with promise rather than with danger. Then the reach tends to

exceed the grasp, and men tend to do better than they have supposed themselves capable of doing. Aspirations are enlarged and expectations continue to rise. As a result, man's inclination to work creatively is sustained, and entrepreneurs view the future with enough optimism to increase the scale and the variety of their undertakings. While these expectations are fed by foreign and other examples of modes of living and doing, they are inspired mainly by the rate at which average income rises in a country as its methods of production change. Accordingly, if the growth rate of average income decelerates or sinks to a low or negligible level, expectations may cease to rise and the stimulus of rising aspirations will vanish. A high rate of population growth can virtually swamp the forces making for growth of average income and hence for continuation of expectations at former levels or even at levels that stimulate individual activity and entrepreneurial undertakings.

Our observations regarding the impact of demographic factors on the determinants of average output support the view that demographic factors are essentially not *causes* of increase in the average, but that they rather condition the contributions most of these determinants can make to modernization and the growth of average income. A high rate of population growth is usually unfavorable to modernization and the growth output. (1) It absorbs goods and services that might otherwise be invested in increasing average output. (2) It produces an age structure heavily loaded with persons of unproductive age, the cost of whose training diverts manpower and materials from activities better suited to increase average output. (3) It increases the size of a population and hence the pressure of numbers on a country's physical resources, whatever their form. Differences in the rates at which components of a population grow may be treated as a corollary to (3) in that these differences make difficult the task of spreading out and evening the pressure of numbers upon whatever is relatively fixed in amount.

Some people take exception to this line of argument. For example, it has been asserted that if a population is growing at a very high rate the relative number of persons with a modern outlook will increase faster. But a society's capacity to modernize young persons is very limited, quality is sacrificed to quantity, and the effective rate of progressive change is reduced.

It has also been asserted that a high rate of population growth—nearly 3 percent per year before 1860—facilitated the development of the United States. This overlooks the fact that then little education was required and children could be set to work in agriculture, which continued to spread into unpeopled but fertile territory until near the close of the nineteenth century. This option is no longer open to the populations of underdeveloped countries; either agricultural land is already occupied, or its development is expensive and cultivation depends on initially expensive modern methods. It is even difficult within heavily populated underdeveloped countries to adjust the economy fully to the relative abundance of labor, since so much equipment is imported from countries with high capital-labor ratios and hence disinclined to produce equipment suited to the needs of countries with relatively high overall labor-capital ratios.

There are determinants of modernization that tend to be less sensitive to demographic conditions than the ones mentioned. These conditions indirectly offset either increase of agents of production per capita or growth of productivity per agent of production. A few of these conditions may be described, together with their effects.

1. *The character of the political system.* This system conditions how flexible an economy is, how the composition of Gross National Product responds to changes in the composition of a population's aggregate demand for goods and services, how much freedom innovative entrepreneurs enjoy, and how much incentive there is for members of the labor force to be productive. The character of a political system is largely independent of demographic factors, but rising population pressure may tend to limit individual freedom.

2. *Social mobility.* Freedom to move from one social category to another is essential to economic flexibility. Great differences in rates of natural increase by social group are unfavorable to social mobility because they put a heavier load upon mobility-facilitating mechanisms than they can bear.

3. *Degree of cooperation and amity among groups and classes.* This conditions a society's capacity for minimizing intergroup conflict and coping with the need to adjust to the changes that accompany both modernization and the acceleration of social change in general. While non-demographic circumstances affect cooperation and amity, a high rate of natural increase, interclass differences in natural increase, and consciousness of population pressure in general or in regions tend to be unfavorable to amity and cooperation.

4. *The effectiveness and stability of the rules, institutions, and legal arrangements used to preserve economic, political, and civil order.* These social mechanisms need to be viewed as generally just, legitimate, and administered by legitimately selected personnel; they are essentially independent, therefore, of demographic factors. However when population pressure is great, interclass fertility differences are pronounced, or fertility levels are subject to great variance, the burdens on a society's rules and institutions may prove excessive.

5. *Values that are more favorable to modernization.* Values are largely independent of demographic factors, but values less favorable to modernization tend to persist longer when fertility is relatively high among those that cling to them. Among the values unfavorable to modernization are those high fertility is associated with, for as I explained earlier, high fertility is unfavorable to the conditions making for modernization and growth of average income.

A lower rate of natural increase is generally favorable to modernization and the growth of average income, given that other operative causes of modernization are present. It is desirable also that fertility be relatively low among those unfavorable to modernization, or at least that it not be relatively high. Unfortunately, high fertility tends to be associated with low incomes and the absence of modernization. Accordingly, modernization and income growth depend upon a people's capacity to reduce fertility. If this link between low income and high fertility is not broken, it may become very difficult to increase aggregate output much faster than population.

10.3. DIVIDED WORLD

The world is not *one* but *several*. In 1961 average income in industrialized countries (exclusive of the USSR and Eastern Europe) was about 11 times that in less industrialized countries; in Northern America it was about 29 times that in East and Southeast Asia (exclusive of Japan). These ratios were higher in 1961 than they were in 1938, and they have increased since then. As the data presented below reveal, incomes in most countries are very low. Moreover, conditions associated with relatively low income or high fertility are correlated with each other and constitute a kind of syndrome of what may be called fertility-reinforcing factors. Modernization therefore entails dissipation of this syndrome as well as augmentation of average income, particularly since fertility is high in all low-income countries and unfavorable to income-improvement in such countries.

The problems here are the product of the past nonsynchronization of rates of change in indicators of development. This state of affairs was produced by the precipitate introduction into the social systems of many nations of disrupting foreign agents. There resulted the analogue of ecological disruption attendant upon the introduction into an ecological system of a new species or condition destructive of long continued balance. Man, of course, has been the major disruptive agent. The population problem of a representative underdeveloped country usually exemplifies man's disruptive ecological role, resulting as it has from the introduction of death control unaccompanied by birth control and other conditions of the sort that generated or accompanied slowly falling mortality in the Western world and in Japan. Today, of course, elimination of pronounced international differences in fertility, average income, and degree of modernization is contingent upon diffusion of many elements from the advanced to the underdeveloped countries. Such diffusion is hindered, however, by demographic and other differences that are much greater today than they were a century ago.

Though the underdeveloped world is made up of countries lagging in modernization, it is not homogeneous. Especially significant from an administrative point of view is the fact that around 1965 over three-fifths of the underdeveloped world's population lived in four Asian countries. Even more significant is the fact that density of population in these countries is greatly in excess of that in underdeveloped South America and sub-Saharan Africa, and that there remains little unused arable land for cultivation.

The number of countries describable as developed is subject to arbitrary determination. Should only countries with a Gross National Product per capita of $1550 or over be so described, in 1969 only 16 countries were developed—11 in Europe, two in Northern America, and Australia, New Zealand, and Israel. If the line is drawn at $800, 35 countries are included, among them Japan, U.S.S.R., Argentina, two Chinese city states (Singapore and Hong Kong), and four oil-rich but underdeveloped countries (Libya, Venezuela, Trinidad and Tobago). Of Europe's countries only Yugoslavia, Portugal, and Albania had averages below $800; of Asia's all but three; of Africa's all but Libya (and prospectively South Africa with $710 in 1969); and of South and Middle America all but Venezuela, Trinidad, and Puerto Rico (essentially a part of the United States). Of those included among the 35, only Venezuela, Trinidad, Hong Kong, Singapore, Puerto Rico, Israel, and Libya have relatively high rates of natural increase.

The countries of the underdeveloped world fell into two categories in 1969: (1) those countries with very large populations (China, India, Indonesia, and what was Pakistan) or at least 30 to 100 million inhabitants (Brazil, Nigeria, the Philippines, Thailand, Turkey, Egypt, South Korea); and (2) those countries (at least 37) with 5 million or fewer inhabitants (28 with around 5 to 15 million, and 11 with 15 to 30 million). Perhaps 60 or more of the underdeveloped countries, while modernizable, are too small to transform into fully developed modern economies. Underdeveloped countries also differ greatly in population density. Nearly all countries in Asia and Middle America averaged over 50 persons per square mile in 1960; only six averaged less. In continental

South America, though, only Ecuador averaged more than 50 persons per square mile in 1960. In Africa at least 14 countries averaged about 50 persons or more per square mile, though the average for the whole continent, much of which is not very arable, was only 29.

Underdeveloped countries also differ greatly in geographical extent. Let us use for comparison a unit of 100,000 square kilometers, or 38,610 square miles—roughly one percent of the area of the United States, which is 9,363,000 square kilometers. Only 29 countries include a territory of ten or more such units; 85 include less than five, and 31 less than one. Area limitations may constrain the number of inhabitants that a country can support in comfort, especially in the absence of international trade, and hence prevent full realization of economies of scale at minimum cost instead of at congestion costs.

Most underdeveloped countries suffer from four demographic disadvantages: high rates of population growth, unfavorable age structures, nonoptimum size, and excessive population density. Unfavorable age structures are associated with rates of natural increase of 2 to 3 percent. Hence adults per thousand inhabitants are at least one-eighth lower in most of the underdeveloped world than in the developed world, and children under 15 per thousand are about 50 percent higher. This age structure not only reduces potential productivity per capita greatly, it also limits capacity to raise their educational levels to parity with those of advanced countries where in 1967 first- and second-level school enrollment was over twice as high as that in Asia and Africa and nearly two-fifths above that in Latin America. It is more difficult, of course, even under otherwise similar conditions, to maintain high educational levels when populations are predominantly rural, and in the underdeveloped world something like three-quarters were still rural in 1970. Because educational levels are so much lower quantitatively and qualitatively in underdeveloped countries their capacities to exploit agricultural and industrial resources and to adapt modern technology to their needs remain very limited, as reflected in their slower relative growth of output per head between the mid-1950s and the late 1960s.

The size of a country's population, and its average income tend to *condition* a country's capacity for exploiting its resources and labor force, but this depends upon many other conditions. There is little or no correlation between size and Gross National Product per head among the world's 20 most populous countries, and no correlation between this average and size of population among the 20 countries (exclusive of Libya, Israel, and Puerto Rico) ranking highest in GNP per head in 1969. Of these 20 countries the U.S. and the U.S.S.R., with populations over 200 million, rank first and last; five, with 50 to 102 million, rank fifth to eighteenth; six, with 10 to 21 million, rank fourth to nineteenth; and seven, with 3 to 8 million, rank second to eighteenth. In 1969 aggregate GNP in these countries ranged from $5.3 billion (in 1964 dollars) in New Zealand to $732.3 billion in the United States. Of the 43 countries in Africa, only well-developed South Africa had a higher aggregate than New Zealand; of the 22 underdeveloped countries in Latin America, only populous Brazil and Mexico; of the 32 underdeveloped countries in Asia and Oceania, only very populous China, India, Indonesia, Pakistan, Turkey, and the Philippines. As a rule size of markets in the underdeveloped world depends mainly upon numbers of inhabitants instead of upon average income. In developed countries average income plays the major role.

Few of the underdeveloped countries are likely to overcome their disadvantage in the same way the countries of Europe have, which overcame limitations upon internal markets and economies of scale through exportation, mainly to other European countries. In 1964, for example, West European countries sent about 65 percent of their exports to Western Europe, and another 17 percent to other developed areas. In 1970 free Europe sent about seven-tenths of its exports to free Europe, and much of the rest to other developed countries. In that same year developed market economies took 77 percent of the exports of such economies and about 74 percent of those of underdeveloped market economies; meanwhile the latter took only about one-fifth of the exports of such underdeveloped economies. Trade among the countries of free Europe not only supported economies of scale directly, especially in small countries, but by increasing average income gave indirect impetus to such economies. Trade among members of the underdeveloped world is constrained by their limited complementarity to one another and, in some degree, by their relative situations. They have not yet developed to the point where the growth of one sustains that of others in the measure that is true of Europe.

A number of conditions may restrict the contributions of external trade to the development of most underdeveloped countries. First, the slow growth of population in the developed world may slacken the expansion of its demand for agricultural and nonmineral products, even in the absence of such protectionist policies as exist in the developed world. Second, change in the character of industry and the structure of the world economy may prove unfavorable. Since the rate of growth of demand for primary products is limited, conditions operative in the supply of manufactures and services become increasingly important. Today the role of human capital and technological superiority in the determination of comparative advantage in exports is growing, particularly in respect of sophisticated products with appeal to high-income populations and of products that embody a great deal of human capital and technology. Underdeveloped countries need therefore to bridge the cultural gap that separates them from advanced countries even as they must bridge the fertility gap.

Large underdeveloped countries are better able than small ones to adjust their economies to the demands of advanced countries, because they have a comparative advantage in the production of labor-oriented goods and services and they can attract large international corporations, together with the accompanying technology, capital, and skilled managerial personnel. In time they can do as Japan has done—namely, adopt and adapt advanced production functions. Small underdeveloped countries need to overcome their smallness, especially smallness that miniaturization of equipment cannot alleviate enough to permit realization of economies of scale even in the absence of much external trade. Entry into free-trade federations conducive to intercountry complementarity can provide considerable access to economies of scale, especially if coupled with cost minimization. Tourism may also contribute significantly, since it is labor oriented.

10.4. THE PAST

The current situation is an outgrowth of the past. The recent increase in international economic inequality is the continuation of a trend: In 1860, L. J. Zimmerman estimates, the poorest half of the world's population earned 26.7 percent of world income; by 1960 it earned only 10 percent. This trend runs counter to that toward greater equality experienced *within* many advanced countries, though it is in keeping with the trend toward greater inequality in underdeveloped countries when they are undergoing modernization.

The joint occurrence of two kinds of change is responsible for this increase in international income inequality. (1) Over the past two centuries technological and related developments have greatly increased man's potential productive capacity. (2) More productive methods tend to spread from the point of origin, but they do so slowly and still remain largely confined to a minor fraction of the world's population, with the result that the economic distance separating rich from poor nations continues to increase.

International inequality is as old as man's literate history, though data pertaining to the degree of it are limited. There was already much inequality in 1700, when average income was fairly close to subsistence in much of the world and much above subsistence only in several European countries. In England and Wales in 1700 the average, according to Phyllis Deane's estimates, was between £8 and £9, the rough equivalent of £47 to £53 as of 1950 when the Indian average approximated £25 and the incomes of a number of Latin American countries were around £70. While the English average may have been slightly below the Dutch in 1700, it approximated the Dutch by 1750, and it exceeded the French average appreciably; because by 1750 it rose to £12 to £13 and to £22 by 1800, increasing in real terms about one-fifth between 1700 and 1750 and about three-fifths between 1700 and 1800. This rise reflects the operation of the forces underlying the Industrial Revolution in England, forces largely offset by population growth until after 1785 when output per capita began to grow nearly 9 percent per decade. Even so, population growth must have slowed the rise of average income, for the birth rate did not begin to decline until after the 1870s even though the death rate had been declining.

Prior to the seventeenth century average output grew very slowly. Growth was intermittent and subject to setbacks, since the basis of man's activity was mainly biological in nature and hence subject to unavoidable adversity. That the pace of growth was low is suggested both by the slowness with which population grew and by the fact that if average output had increased only 2 to 3 percent per decade it would have grown 22 to 34 percent per century and 169 to 338 percent each 500 years. Yet such growth was experienced only when the bourgeoisie were influential or the state undertook productive investment.

Four conditions were immediately responsible for this slow rate of growth. (1) Manpower was ineffectively used, and most men were without incentive, because it was a world in which the stick rather than the carrot was depended upon for motivation. As late as 1810 a writer in the *Edinburgh Review* wrote, "The bamboo is the great moral panacea of China." (2) Technology was improved very slowly. (3) Surplus labor power, of which there was considerable, was invested *unproductively*, as a rule, especially after land had been cleared and fitted for agriculture. (4) The pace of growth was set ultimately by agriculture, source of nearly all of man's food and raw materials prior to the nineteenth century, and agriculture progressed very slowly.

Man's disenthrallment from the conditions that impeded growth of income proceeded somewhat differently in England, bellwether of the Industrial Revolution in the West, than in Japan, the only non-European state to undergo modernization. In England agriculture underwent a structural revolution, marked by a decline in the number of agriculturalists and increasing dependence upon agricultural imports purchasable with exports. This revolution, its mainspring being perhaps "deep in the long history of European civilization," had no single origin, according to R. M. Hartwell; rather it reflected "manifestations of growth"—capital accumulation, innovation, population growth, opportunities for profit, specialization, shifts in the structure of the economy—a cumulative process that transformed the economy in "a relatively short period of time." English agriculture responded to these same forces at a much lower rate than nonagricultural output, and not enough to match population growth, but enough to allow free rein to an agricultural revolution dependent on imported cotton.

Japan's experience was different from England's; what is more, according to S. Ishikawa it is not very applicable to other densely populated Asian lands. In Japan agricultural output grew, in part because the rural population continued to increase until World War I; it grew in response to the progress of industrialization and supplied industries with labor, capital, food, and raw materials. Japan's agriculture could play this role because in the early nineteenth century it was already equipped with infrastructure (such as irrigation) and could rely upon improvements in seed, fertilizer, and the like. Thus between 1878–1880 and 1918–1920 yield per acre of grain increased about 70 percent (whereas in India there was no upward trend), and between 1918–1920 and 1961–1963 it increased another 42 percent.

Population growth was generally held in check in pre-1700 Europe by high mortality and social and other controls, among them the contraceptive method mentioned in the Bible and by Herodotus. The Black Death removed much of the growth that took place in Europe after 1000, thus relieving localized population pressures; it also, J. C. Russell believes, prompted some relaxation, initially in Italy, of population controls such as taboos on marriage, especially early marriage. This state of reduced control over population growth probably continued with the rise of nationalism and the populationist views of mercantilist theorists and administrators. Even so population grew slowly by modern standards, hardly 0.5 percent per year between 1650 and 1850 and somewhat less between 1550 and 1650, held in check by mortality and curbs on natality. Japan suffered from population pressure in the seventeenth century when numbers grew about 0.33 percent per year. As a result population growth was controlled and numbers grew very little between 1700 and 1850, and only 0.8 percent per year between 1850 and 1900, when modernization was getting under way.

The demographic situation in Western Europe before the mid-eighteenth century was quite different from that in the underdeveloped countries of Asia, Africa, and Latin America since (say) 1940. Population grew very slowly in pre-industrial Europe, limited by the food supply held in check by the lack of increase of yields and crop acreage. As Phyllis Deane observes, when population rose product per head fell, and when output rose population grew and eventually leveled out earlier gains in income. Europe's age composition was favorable in that low life expectancy and high infant mortality, combined with a birth rate under 40, tended to result in a population with about 63 to 64 percent in the 15–64 age group and only 31 to 32 percent under 15. The corresponding percentages in a stable male population with a life expectancy of about 54 years and a growth rate of about 2.5 percent per year are about 56 and 41. In 1960 the corresponding percentages for the sexes combined was 56 and 41 in South Asia, 54 and 43 in Africa, 55 and 42 in Latin America, and 64 and 30 in Japan.

The forces that made for economic development in England and later Europe in and after the eighteenth century and in Japan after the Meiji Restoration were not held in check by demographic conditions nearly so much as in today's underdeveloped world. Therefore neither country, not even densely populated Japan, can serve as a universal model for densely populated Asian countries. Here, as Ishikawa points out, agricultural output per head has been held down by a shortage of required infrastructure, with the result that agriculture has not proved capable of supporting development as it did in Japan. Moreover, capital has not been forthcoming in amounts necessary to facilitate effective employment of a growing population under conditions of modern capital intensity. Development programs need therefore be fitted to conditions current in countries, but always with major emphasis upon control of population growth.

10.5. THE WAY OUT

The demographic situation in many underdeveloped countries may be viewed as an outgrowth of the selective incidence of elements of European culture, elements that failed to strengthen and in some instances weakened indigenous controls on fertility and population growth. With the development of new, quick-acting, inexpensive, and effective methods of death control, especially after World War I, earlier demographic equilibria were upset, because fertility could not be and was not brought down commensurately, and the rate of population growth rose to two to three or more times what it was in Europe between 1800 and 1950.

Had enough of the elements of Western culture or analogous elements of Japanese culture been assimilated into the cultures of today's underdeveloped countries, the demographic obstacles they now confront would have been much smaller, because their natality and mortality would have responded to such development as took place, with natality trending downward in the wake of such decline in mortality as took place and in reaction to changes in the diverse factors that condition fertility by country and social group. While the resulting balance between natality and mortality might have resembled those in the underdeveloped world between (say) 1850 and 1920, it would have been succeeded by much less of an upsurge in natural increase than subsequently took place—by a rate both closer to one than to 2 or more percent and already in the process of decline. Since vital rates did not evolve in this fashion, their modernization, and that of underdeveloped economies, entails a redressing of the adverse effects of nonsynchronization of natality and mortality trends in the past century.

The need for such redress is illustrated in figures provided by the United States Bureau of the Census. These indicate how population will grow by 2070 if the Net Reproduction Rate remains at the 1970 level. A few examples follow:

Country	N.R.R.	Population	Millions	Area (in million sq. mi.)	Inhabitants (per sq. mi.)	
Brazil	2.30	3504	(238)	3286	1067	(29)
Mexico	2,49	2233	(135)	762	2927	(65)
Venezuela	2.50	420	(27)	352	1193	(29)
Ghana	2.17	410	(22)	92	4456	(94)
Morocco	2.75	1505	(45)	172	8750	(37)
U.A.R.	2.26	1237	(81)	387	3196	(83)
China	1.95	20,850	(1661)	3620	5760	(200)
India	2.09	25,418	(1451)	1262	20,141	(426)
Indonesia	1.93	4507	(275)	576	7825	(203)
Iran	2.71	2532	(81)	636	4000	(44)
Thailand	2.53	1490	(93)	198	7525	(177)
Turkey	2.26	1189	(83)	301	3950	(114)

The figures in the last column indicate the number of inhabitants per square mile in 2070 should the N.R.R. not change (the 1969 density figures are in parentheses). The 2070 densities indicate a population per acre ranging from nearly two in Brazil and Venezuela to over 30 in India. The ratio per cultivable acre would be much higher, since a considerable fraction of the area of any country is not cultivable or has been diverted to other uses. For example about half of India's acres are arable, but only about one-fourth of the world's acres are potentially arable. Should the N.R.R. descend to 1.0 by 1990–1995 and populations become stationary around 2050, they would approximate the figures in parentheses. Should the N.R.R. not descend to 1.0 until 2000–2005, populations would become stationary around 2060 and would be about 20 to 25 percent larger than reported in the parentheses.

Problems associated with sheer pressure of numbers on territory, to be distinguished from those associated with a high rate of natural increase, vary greatly in the underdeveloped world, as suggested by the 1969 density figures in parentheses in the last column. In 1960 in the underdeveloped world, regions of low density including 494 million population averaged 4 to 20 person per square kilometer; the corresponding average in regions of medium density numbering 1480 million people ranged from 49 to 85; it approximated 181 in regions of high density where 47 million people lived.

A more significant measure of density is the number of potentially arable acres per inhabitant. In 1965 these ranged from 0.84 in Asia and 0.97 in Europe to 8.53 in South America and 27.2 in Australia and New Zealand. Since only one of the world's 2.38 potentially arable acres has been cultivated, it might be possible to double the world's acreage under cultivation. Moreover, if it became possible, with the help of adequate irrigation, to make full use of multiple cropping, the world's acreage might be raised to the equivalent of close to 16 billion *single-crop* acres, at least double the world's estimated arable land area. Accordingly, if effective acreage and yield per acre can each be tripled, the world's food supply may be susceptible of increase by a factor of nine or ten. Even then, should numbers and food consumption per capita augment total consumption by 2 to 3 percent per year, world food requirements would match this potential within about a century. So great an increase of food output is unlikely, however, if only because so much underexploited land lies outside densely populated countries and the latter are likely to lack the means to import food.

The most important measure for modernization and the elevation of average income in underdeveloped countries is reduction of the Net Reproduction Rate to 1.0 within the next 30 to 40 years, since even then population will finally be 2.5 to 3.0 or more times as large as it was in 1970. Moreover, the age structure will evolve slowly in a productive direction if fertility declines slowly rather than rapidly. If fertility is to be reduced rapidly, it will not suffice to diffuse effective family planning methods much more rapidly than at present. It will also be necessary to facilitate this by restructuring the relevant penalty-reward and cost-benefit structures in underdeveloped countries until the Gross Reproduction Rate descends to a level compatible with an N.R.R. of 1.0. Of particular importance is the absorption of women into the labor force;

then women have an alternative to child bearing and unattractive house-hold chores, and the opportunity cost of children is greatly increased by the loss of income that childbearing entails. Investment in required "socio-economic" restructuring and encouragement of sterilization yield very high returns.

Also of great importance is rapid increase in urban employment, since then labor-saving and other forms of agricultural progress will be stimu-lated and ever larger fractions of the population will reside in milieus favorable to fertility control. Continuation of this urbanization process is dependent upon high investment in both the development of jobs in urban centers and the modernization of agriculture so that the agricul-tural fraction of the labor force may be reduced, eventually, to something like 15 to 20 percent. Moreover, since *productive* urban populations do not, as a rule, easily grow more than 4 percent per year, it is essential that both rural and urban natural increase be kept low, say not above one percent. Otherwise reduction of the agricultural population in rela-tive and absolute size will proceed too slowly, and increase in output per agriculturalist will not be sufficient to supply the aggregate demand of an urban population growing in numbers and average income, with the result that food costs will rise and demands of urban workers for higher monetary wages may trigger off price inflation.

Third, as already indicated, a high rate of savings and investment in physical capital and a satisfactory rate of investment in personal capital are essential if the required amount of urban employment and agricul-tural progress are to be made possible and sufficiently advanced tech-nologies are to be introduced from abroad and adapted to domestic needs. So high a rate of savings is not possible unless the rate of natural increase is pushed down to at least one percent.

Fourth, conditions of international exchange must be improved. Many underdeveloped countries need to engage in the export of manufactures as well as in that of raw materials and agricultural products; otherwise they cannot earn enough foreign exchange to finance internal economic development. Foreign aid and investment can complement and supple-ment these sources of exchange, particularly given that one percent of GNP in the developed world roughly approximates 5 percent of that of the underdeveloped world; but it cannot contribute notably in the absence of heavy domestic investment. Both aid and investment are most effective when the rate of population growth is low and when, as a result, investment-discouraging political instability is not too likely to thrive on excessive poverty and frustration.

Fifth, though a few underdeveloped countries now have large enough populations or average incomes or both to give release to economies of scale and economies associated with optimum population distribution, most are too small in numbers and markets. Only through international trade, as individuals or within customs or other trading unions, can these countries partially surmount limitations imposed by their smallness even should miniaturization of plant size somewhat relax these limitations. Should some countries find larger populations preferable, these may most economically be achieved through low rates of population growth, say in the neighborhood of one percent, for then the availability of capital and manpower for productive activity is not likely to be unduly reduced.

The burden of the argument in this chapter is not that modernization and economic development have their origin in demographic conditions, or that the countries composing the underdeveloped world are so nearly alike in degree or stage of development that similar policies are indicated. The burden is rather that development is a historical process, the product of evolution through time, and hence, despite conditions common to most if not all underdeveloped countries, a process varying somewhat from country to country. At the same time it is evident that a high rate of population growth is unfavorable to modernization even if the population of a country is describable as suboptimal in size; then gradual growth, say at a rate of around one percent, may be indicated. Because population growth can be a deterrent to modernization, it needs to be brought under effective control. This can be accomplished by making the means of contraception available everywhere and by restructuring the motivational milieu surrounding individuals and families in such wise as to ensure adequate use of the means.

A great deal is being published these days on most of the subjects covered in this little volume. In what follows selected sources are indicated. Many fine studies have been published by the Population Council, 245 Park Avenue, New York, New York.

1. POPULATION GROWTH AND DISTRIBUTION

The United Nations provides a great deal of current information on all regions of the world in the *Demographic Yearbook*, the *Population Bulletin*, a series of studies under the general title *Population Studies*, and reports by its regional commissions, the Food and Agricultural Organization. Information on many countries may be found in W. S. and E. S. Woytinsky, *World Population and Production* (New York: Twentieth Century Fund, 1953); two works of Simon Kuznets, *Economic Growth of Nations* (Cambridge: Harvard University Press, 1971) and *Modern Economic Growth: Rate, Structure, and Spread* (New Haven: Yale University Press, 1966); D. V. Glass and D. E. C. Eversley, eds., *Population in History* (Chicago: Aldine, 1965); M. K. Bennett, *The World's Food* (New York: Harper, 1954). Information on the United States is easily accessible in publications of the U. S. Bureau of the Census, *U. S. Statistical Abstract* and in *Current Population Reports*, especially in Series P-20, P-23, P-25, and P-60. Several monographs published in 1958 by Wiley (New York) review America's growth: Conrad and Irene B. Taeuber, *The Changing Population of the United States;* W. H. Grabill, *et al., The Fertility of American Women;* P. C. Glick, *American Families,* and E. P. Hutchinson, *Immigrants and Their Children, 1850–1950;* also monographs based on the 1960 Census. On fertility see U. S. Bureau of the Census, *The Two-Child Family and Population Growth: An International View* (Sept. 1971).

On stable populations see A. J. Coale and Paul Demeny, *Regional Life Tables and Stable Populations* (Princeton: Princeton University Press, 1966); on urbanization, Kingsley Davis, *World Urbanization, 1950–1970,* (Berkeley: Institute of International Studies, University of California, 1969-).

2. POPULATION AND THE NATURAL ENVIRONMENT

This topic is now being treated at length, usually in connection with population problems. For information see Sterling Brewbaker, *To Live*

Bibliography

on Earth: Man and His Environment in Perspective (Baltimore: Johns Hopkins Press, 1972); Paul R. Ehrlich, John P. Holdren, and R. W. Holm, eds., *Man and the Ecosphere* (San Francisco: Freeman, 1971); Economic Commission for Europe, *ECE Symposium on Problems Relating to Environment* (New York: United Nations, 1971); John P. Holdren and Paul Ehrlich, eds., *Global Ecology* (New York: Harcourt, 1971); *The World Food Problem*, a Report of the President's Science Advisory Committee, The White House (Washington, D. C., 1967); *Restoring the Quality of Our Environment*, Report of the President's Science Advisory Committee, The White House (Washington, D.C., 1965); Lorus and Margery Milne, *Patterns of Survival* (Englewood Cliffs: Prentice-Hall, 1967); A. J. Lotka, *Elements of Physical Biology* (Baltimore: Williams and Wilkins, 1925); S. F. Singer, ed., *Is There an Optimum Level of Population* (New York: McGraw-Hill, 1971); National Academy of Sciences, *Resources and Man* (San Francisco: Freeman, 1969); Stuart Mudd, ed., *The Population Crisis and the Use of World Resources* (The Hague: W. Junk, 1964); S. L. Udall, *The Quiet Crisis* (New York: Holt, 1963); L. B. Lave and E. P. Seskin, "Air Pollution and Human Health," *Science* (Aug. 21, 1970), pp. 723–33.

3. AGE COMPOSITION

Changes in age composition produce various effects. Some of these are discussed in several of the United Nations *Population Studies* referred to in Section 1 of this bibliography; D. J. Bogue, *Principles of Demography* (New York: Wiley, 1969); W. G. Bowen and T. A. Finegan, *The Economics of Labor Force Participation* (Princeton: Princeton University Press, 1969); Michael Brennan, *et al.*, *The Economics of Age* (New York: Norton, 1967); J. Black, "A Note on the Economics of National Superannuation," *Economic Journal*, LXVIII (June 1958), 338–53; Juanita M. Kreps, *Lifetime Allocation of Work and Income* (Durham: Duke University Press, 1971).

4. POPULATION GROWTH, NET EFFECTS, POPULATION OPTIMA

These topics are all touched upon in a number of the works cited earlier. Costs and effects are treated in a symposium on "Population and Environment in the United States," *American Economic Review, Papers and Proceedings*, LXXI (2), (May 1971), 392–421; J. J. Spengler, *Declining Population Growth Revisited*, Monograph 14, 1971, Carolina Population Center, (Chapel Hill, N. C.); E. F. Denison, *Why Growth Rates Differ: Postwar Differences in Nine Western Countries* (Washington, D. C.: The Brookings Institution, 1967). On optima see Singer, ed., *Is There an Optimum Level of Population;* Alfred Sauvy, *General Theory of Population* (New York: Basic Books, 1969); Daniel O. Price, ed., *The 99th Hour* (Chapel Hill: University of North Carolina Press, 1967); J. J. Spengler, *Population Economics* (Durham: Duke University Press, 1972); J. J. Spengler and Otis Dudley Duncan, eds., *Population Theory and Policy* and *Demographic Analysis* (Glencoe: Free Press, 1956); Colin Clark, *Population Growth and Land Use* (New York: St. Martins, 1967); Harvey Leibenstein, *A Theory of Economic-Demographic Development* (Princeton: Princeton University Press, 1954); A. J. Coale, ed., *Demographic and Economic Change in Developed Countries* (Princeton: Princeton University Press, 1960); Goran Ohlin, *Population Control and Economic Development* (Paris: OECD, 1967); Walter Isard, *Methods of Regional Analysis: An Introduction to Regional Science* (New York: Wiley, 1960).

5. POPULATION POLICY

Population policy is touched upon in some of the works cited in Section 4. Especially useful also are Philip Handler, ed., *Biology and the Future of Man* (New York: Oxford, 1970); National Academy of Sciences, *Rapid Population Growth: Consequences and Policy Implications* (Baltimore: Johns Hopkins Press, 1971); C. A. Doxiadis, "Ekistics, The Science of Human Settlements," *Science* (Oct. 23, 1970), pp. 393–404; J. G. Williamson, "Regional Inequality and the Process of National Development," *Economic Development and Cultural Change* XIII, Part 2, (July 1965); Marion Clawson, *Suburban Land Conversion in the United States* (Baltimore: Johns Hopkins Press, 1971); Gunnar Myrdal, *Asian Drama* (New York: Twentieth Century Fund, 1968). A. J. Coale and E. M. Hoover, *Population Growth and Economic Development in Low-Income Countries* (Princeton: Princeton University Press, 1958). Many aspects of policy are treated in a series of studies released in 1972 by the United States Population Commission, Washington, D. C.

6. ECONOMIC DEVELOPMENT, PAST AND PROSPECTIVE

Since 1940 a vast literature on modernization, economic development, and economic growth has come into existence, and a variety of data and other information has been compiled by the United Nations and its regional commissions, and the World Bank and the International Monetary Fund. Besides materials referred to earlier, the *Cambridge Economic History of Europe* (Cambridge: Cambridge University Press, 1942), and

Simon Kuznets's many studies of economic growth, I have also used made of the following: Phyllis Deane, *The First Industrial Revolution,* (Cambridge: Cambridge University Press, 1965); Phyllis Deane and W. C. Cole, *British Economic Growth, 1688–1959* (Cambridge: Cambridge University Press, 1962); E. F. Denison, *Sources of Economic Growth in the United States* (New York: Committee for Economic Development, 1962); R. M. Hartwell, "The Causes of the Industrial Revolution," *Economic History Review,* XVIII (August 1965), 164–82; S. Ishikawa, *Economic Development in Asian Perspective* (Tokyo: Kinokuniya, 1967). The history of population growth has been dealt with by M. K. Bennett, Colin Clark, John Durand, and Josiah C. Russell, among others. Especially useful here is D. V. Glass and D. E. C. Eversley, eds., *Population in History* (Chicago: Aldine, 1965). Some of the issues raised in this chapter are dealt with in a developed-country setting in the Report of the Commission On Population Growth and the American Future (Washington, D.C.: Government Printing Office, 1972), along with background papers. In the early part of this century government reports on population policy usually were motivated by concern at the decline in natality.

Age
    and genius, 118–19
    and obsolescence, 114
    and productivity, 67–68
    and progress, 74, 118–20
    and recreation, 77
    and retirement problems, 34, 72–76,
        118
    and time horizon, 52, 119, 137
Age composition, 2, 18, 63–64, 66, 73, 166
    genesis of, 63–66, 76–77
Age structure. *See also* Age composition
    and dependency, 6, 13, 63, 67–68, 70,
        73–77, 118
    and education, 70–71
    and employment, 71–74
    and equity, 122–24
    and flexibility of economy, 120–22, 124
    and income distribution, 117, 123–24
    and natural increase, 64–67, 73
    and political power, 63, 68, 76–77
    and potential productivity, 63, 67–68,
        73–75, 117–20
    and social security, 72–76, 92, 135
    and youth-connected problems, 63,
        70–72, 123
Agriculture. *See also* Consumption;
        Famine; Land; Water
    and food supply, 6, 20, 24, 44, 46–56,
        58
    and migration, 24–27
    and modernization, 23–25, 50–52, 55,
        153
    and population, 23–28, 38, 49, 53, 56
    and revolution in methods, 6, 24, 42,
        51, 53, 56
    and rural population, 25–27
Amenities, natural, 20, 30
Apparatus and views of state, 33, 34, 97,
        98, 126, 129

Baby boom, 10
Biomass, 143
Biosphere, 43, 44
Birth deficit, 11
Births, unwanted, 134
Black Death, 4, 165
Bourgeoisie, 164

Capital, 13, 39, 82, 131, 166
Cargo cult, 49
Channels, network of, 33–34
Children. *See also* Costs; Cost-benefit
        relations
    costs of, 80, 82–86, 92, 136
    demand for, 92, 95, 136–37, 140, 146
    utility of, 92–95
Cities, 17, 27, 29, 33–37, 41, 52, 169.
        See also Distribution; Economies
    governance of, 34
    network of, 36
    size of, 8, 34, 35, 39–42, 140
    structure of, 139–40
City state, 130
Civilization, European, 112
Communication, 33, 35, 97, 133. *See also*
        Information
Complementarities, 30–32, 37. *See also*
        Economies
Composition of output and population, 2,
        113, 130
Computerization, 33
Concentration of population, 30, 31, 33,
        40, 149
Consumption and consumer goods, 6, 34,
        49, 57, 60, 103, 114, 115, 125.
        See also Agriculture
Contraception, 112, 130, 133, 138, 146,
        168, 170. *See also* Control of
        population growth and distribution
Control of population growth and
        distribution. *See also* Distribution;
        Policy
    grounds for, 36–38, 109, 137, 141–47
    methods, 148–49
    prospects for, 146–49
Cost-benefit relations and population
        growth, 78, 80, 82, 90–94, 109,
        136–37, 140, 146, 168
Costs, 31, 78–95. *See also* Children
    age-structural, 82, 85
    categories, 78–89, 145
    conflict, 82, 89
    decisions, 79, 80
    environmental, 82, 86–88
    living, 83–85
    population density, 82, 88, 89, 91
    socio-economic, 34
    time and physiological, 78, 144–45
Countries of the world, three categories,
        104

175

Adams, Henry, 151
Alexander, 100
Anteus, 44
Aristotle, 97, 100, 130
Augustus Caesar, 1, 111, 142

Bennett, M. K., 7, 171, 174
Black, J., 172
Bogue, D. J., 172
Bonner, James, 56
Bowen, W. G., 172
Brennan, M., 172
Brewbaker, Sterling, 148, 149, 171
Brown, Lester, 55

Cantillon, Richard, 111
Carneiro, R. L., 21
Christ, 1
Clark, Colin, 28, 32, 173, 174
Clawson, M., 173
Coale, A. J., 4, 64, 113, 171, 173
Cole, W. C., 174
Columbus, Christopher, 1

Dalton, Hugh, 105
Davis, Kingsley, 171
Deane, Phyllis, 164, 166, 174
Deevy, E. S., 6
Demeny, Paul, 171
Denison, E. F., 154, 172, 174
Doxiadis, C. A., 139, 173
Dubos, René, 44
Duncan, Otis Dudley, 173
Durand, John, 174

Ehrlich, Paul, 172
Enke, Stephen, 138
Euler, Leonhard, 100
Eversley, D. E. C., 171, 174

Finegan, T. A., 172
Fourastié, Jean, 1

Gerard, R. W., 44
Glass, D. V., 171, 174
Glick, P. C., 171
Grabill, W. H., 171

Hammond, R. P., 60

Handler, Philip, 173
Hartwell, R. M., 165, 174
Herodotus, 165
Holdren, J. P., 172
Holm, R. W., 172
Homer, 1
Hoover, E. M., 173
Hutchinson, E. P., 171

Isard, Walter, 173
Ishikawa, I., 165, 166, 174

Johnson, Harry, 82

Keynes, J. M., 125, 150
Kreps, J. M., 172
Kuznets, Simon, 19, 171, 174

Lave, L. B., 87, 172
Leibenstein, Harvey, 173
Leibniz, G. W. von, 100
Lotka, A. J., 43, 45, 46, 141, 148, 172

Malthus, T. R., 91, 130
Mehta J. K., 128
Meiji, 166
Mill, J. S., 19, 87, 101, 127
Milne, Loris, 172
Milne, Margery, 172
Mudd, Stuart, 172
Myrdal, G., 173

Nisbet, R. A., 110

Ohlin, Goran, 173

Pearl, Raymond, 78
Pennock, Jean L., 83, 84
Piddington, R. A., 46
Plato, 1, 97, 100, 130
Polo, Marco, 39
Polybius, 1
Pope, Alexander, 152
Price, Daniel O., 173

Ricardo, David, 19
Robinson E. A. G., 98
Russell, J. C., 165, 174

Sauvy, Alfred, 173
Seskin, E. P., 87, 172

INDEX OF PERSONS

Africa, 7, 9, 10, 18, 19, 50, 54, 73, 133, 161, 162, 165
Africa, South, 162
Alaska, 58
Amazon, 58
America. *See* United States
America, Latin, 7, 9, 18, 19, 40, 161, 165, 166
America, Middle, 9, 160
America, North, 9, 54, 58, 133
America, Northern, 8, 73, 100, 132, 152, 159, 160
America, South, 9, 54, 133, 152, 160, 161, 162, 168
Asia, 7, 9, 10, 19, 38, 40, 50, 51, 52, 54, 56, 112, 133, 152, 159–62, 165, 168
Asia, East, 17
Athens, 47
Australia, 9, 40, 50, 54, 100, 104, 122, 129, 133, 152, 160, 168
Austria, 12

Brazil, 160, 162, 167
Brittany, 139
Bulgaria, 77

Canada, 58, 104
Caribbean Region, 9
Ceylon, 12
Chile, 12
China, 10, 45, 105, 142, 152, 160, 162, 167
Constantinople, 39

Denmark, 12

Ecuador, 161
Egypt, 12, 160
England and Wales, 12, 19, 20, 26, 139, 166
Europe, 4, 9, 11, 17, 26, 27, 36, 40, 50, 72, 73, 100, 101, 132, 133, 139, 152, 160, 162, 165, 166, 168
Europe, Eastern, 11, 12, 132, 159
Europe, Overseas, 100
Europe, Western, 11, 12, 19, 56, 63, 68, 100, 112, 142, 165

INDEX OF PLACES

Finland, 139
France, 11, 12, 26, 72, 129

Germany, East, 77
Ghana, 167
Great Britain, 72

Hangchow, 39
Hellas, 9
Holland, 36
Hong Kong, 160

India, 10, 19, 45, 51, 55, 105, 142, 152, 160, 162, 167
Indonesia, 142, 152, 167
Iran, 167
Ireland, 138, 139
Israel, 99, 160, 161
Italy, 47, 165

Jamaica, 12
Japan, 10, 56, 59, 100, 105, 118, 132, 152, 159, 160, 163, 165, 166

Korea, 10
Kuwait, 103

Libya, 100, 160, 161
London, 39, 40

Manchuria, 10
Mediterranean World, 100
Mesopotamia, 45
Mexico, 12, 162, 167
Middle East, 38
Morocco, 167

Netherlands, 12, 76
New York City, 84
New Zealand, 50, 100, 133, 152, 160, 162, 168
Nigeria, 160
Norway, 6

Pakistan, 10, 105, 152, 159, 160, 162
Paris, 40
Peking, 39
Philippines, 160, 162
Puerto Rico, 160, 161

Rio Grande, 9
Roman Empire, 6, 7, 97